WHY I KNOW THAT YOU DO NOT LOVE YOUR CHILDREN!

This book is for anybody who has an open mind and is intrigued about the controversial and secret theories behind the world we live in. We need to over-stand the truth of this world in order to guide our children and our future to make this world a better place.

This book has an informal feel and is very funny, factual and addictive. The author Dr Kwadw(o) Naya: Baa Ankh Em Ra A'lyun Eil opens our eyes to the truth(s) behind the new digitalized society in which we live in.

A courageous person is not a fool; they are a successful man or woman who does what **THEY WANT** to **ACHIEVE THEIR GOALS**. **REMEMBER**, people who have no **GOALS**, have **NO WAY, NO PURPOSE**. If we teach our **CHILDREN** to **CONFORM** to a **FAILING SYSTEM** or **SOCIETY,** then **WE** have **FAILED** already. **WE ARE THE POWER.**

– Dr Kwadw(o) Naya: Baa Ankh Em Ra A'lyun Eil

WHY I KNOW THAT YOU DO NOT LOVE YOUR CHILDREN!

What every parent should know.

Dr Kwadw(o) Naya: Baa Ankh
Em Ra A'lyun Eil

Published by: Golden Child Promotions Publishing Company

All the proceeds of this book will be donated to The Golden Child Promotions Charity, to fund youth development.

https://goldenchildpromotions.co.uk

Thank You

Scroll 1: The Fuzzy Logic Series

Published 2019 by Golden Child Promotions Publishing Ltd.

Portland House,

Belmont Business Park,

Durham,

DH1 1TW

9x9x9@goldenchildpromotionspublishing.co.uk

Revised Second Edition

READ THIS FIRST

Download Why I Know That You Do Not Love Your Children! Ebook FREE!

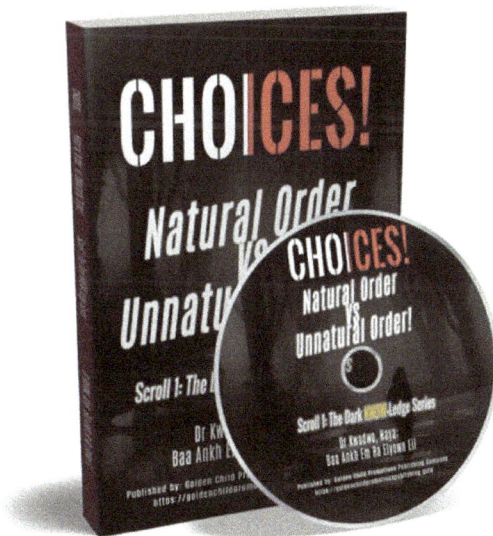

WHY I KNOW THAT YOU DO NOT LOVE YOUR CHILDREN!

Dr Kwadw(o) Naya: Baa Ankh Em Ra A'Iyun Eil

What is really going on in this world? I thought I knew the answer to that question a long time ago, but it is only coming to me now, after 43 years. The world is changing, and our lives are changing dramatically. We are going into a new era called "The Information Age," where traditional values are being phased out and replaced with computers and technology that have been changing our minds unconsciously. What is really going on and what can we do about it?

I have found out so many things the hard way; please don't make the same mistake(s) as me.

WHY I KNOW THAT YOU DO NOT LOVE YOUR CHILDREN!

The world is changing around us. What is happening and what can we do about it?

Dr Kwadw(o) Naya: Baa Ankh
Em Ra A'lyun Eil

GCP Publishing Ltd

ACKNOWLEDGMENTS

I would like to give my THANKS AND ACKNOWLED-GMENTS to eight great people who helped me bring this work to fruition:

Axel Williamson, Betty Davis and Tramaine Williamson, thank you for having the patience to read my work while in its rough phases. You were the only ones there for me during this time and I will never forget that; your feedback was crucial.

I would also like to thank and acknowledge the great works of Hayley, Hans and Stephen: Hayley and Hans for their fantastic editing and Stephen for the book cover design. It took us many concepts before we could agree on the right book cover design, but he had the patience and diligence to see everything through, which I truly appreciate. Also, big thanks and love to hansbarrow with the excellent job he did with the formatting.

My biggest and most heartfelt tribute, acknowledgement and appreciation goes to Alicia McKenzie who painstakingly and most kindly taken care of the audio book in between her hectic schedule. I could never be more thankful. Thank you.

DEDICATION

"I would like to dedicate this book to my *DAUGHTER & GRANDSON*. I would also like to dedicate it to *KAYDEN, FARRAH* and *JAXX* (You know who you are). Hopefully, they can *LEARN* something and *NOT* make the same *MISTAKES* as I had." – Dr Kwadw(o) Naya: Baa Ankh Em Ra A'lyun Eil

This book will not be very popular.

Many people will not appreciate the content.

Many people will not like the content.

Many people will think that I am a fool or a conspiracy nut.

But if you do manage to read this publication in its entirety and you still **THINK** and **ACT** the same...

...then maybe you do not have love for your **CHILDREN**? Not **DIVINE LOVE**?

Do you know what **DIVINE LOVE IS**?

Or maybe I am a fool or a conspiracy nut, who knows?

CONTENTS

INTRODUCTION

28th December 2018 @ 01:06 I am sat her thinking:

WHAT IS GOING ON IN THIS WORLD? WHAT IS REALLY GOING ON? DO WE NOT LOVE OUR CHILDREN ANYMORE?

Am I the only crazy person in this world, or the only sane one? Who knows? I guess you will have to let me know!

What I do know is that our children are the future; without them, there will be no future.

What would happen if there were no new babies crying?

We are all masters of our **WORLD(S)** and **ENVIRONMENTS**; we create what we want, that I know.

We have created our children in our own image and have shaped the world accordingly.

Is it a nice world that we have created?

I don't feel so, and I hope my Daughter is reading this now.

Our children are the **GOLDEN ONES;** we need to know that. We should live for them as they should live for us, in accordance with **NATURE,** not **MAN**.

THE LAWS OF NATURE **NOT** MAN.

THE LAWS OF **MAAT**!

It would appear that we do not have **DIVINE LOVE** for our children because if we did, we would not do the things that we do.

CHAPTER 1:

NEEDS

I have learned a lot in my life, but I still feel like a fool.

You see, the more I learn, the more I realize that I don't know anything, not on the grand scheme of things.

I have had the opportunity to have a lot of invaluable experiences which have shaped and molded me into the **being** that I am today.

I am still a fool but a much wiser fool than the day before.

I left school when I was 15 years old, with no qualifications, and decided a few years later that I would like to learn business as I felt it may be a way forward.

I somehow managed to coerce myself onto a business course: A Certificate & Diploma in Business & Management with NEBSM. One of the first things that they taught me was a managerial concept which I am sure you have all heard of. It is quite an old, dated concept now.

It was a theory brought about by Maslow's study into human motivation and psychology – called Maslow's Hierarchy of Needs:

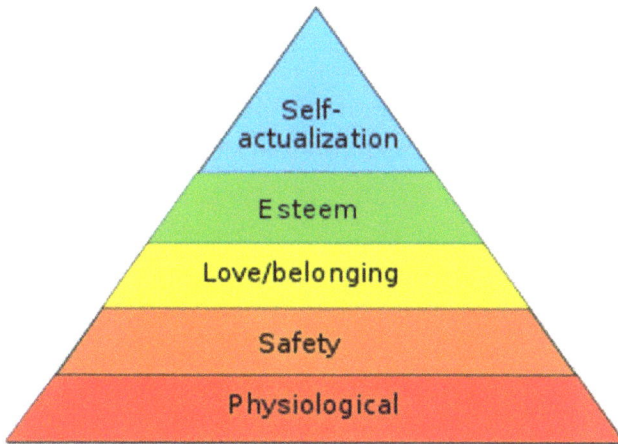

Maslow's hierarchy of needs represented as a pyramid with the more basic needs at the bottom.

Maslow's hierarchy of needs is a theory in *psychology* proposed by *Abraham Maslow* in his 1943 paper "A Theory of Human Motivation."[1] The theory is used to study how humans are motivated.

Let us have a look at what he has noted; we can start from the most basic needs:

(1)   PHYSIOLOGICAL NEEDS – (Food, Water, Sleep, Shelter, Sex)

I agree with Maslow here. I feel that these are our basic requirements for human motivation. These are

---

[1] Maslow, A. H. (1943). A theory of human motivation. *Psychological Review.* Page 375.

the things that we need to get right to motivate our children and ourselves.

Do we give our children the right food? The right water? Do they get enough sleep or go to bed at the right times? Are their sleeping patterns and routines structured? Have we spoken to them about **SEX**? If not, who is going to give them that knowledge? Some dirty old man or woman?

(2)   **SAFETY – (**_Personal Security, Emotional Security, Financial Security, Health and Well-being_**, Safety Needs against Accidents and Illness)**

This speaks for itself, really. We all need to stay **SAFE,** and I am sure that we would like our **CHILDREN** to be safe on **ALL** levels — from personal to emotional security.

(3)   LOVE/BELONGING – (Family, Friendships and Intimacy)

Our children need nurturing and guiding through their life. A child is for **LIFE**. Even when we are grown, **WE** still need love and guidance.

Our children are the next generation, how can they be expected to **LOVE** if they have never been **LOVED?** How can we expect them to **LOVE PROPERLY** if they have never been **LOVED PROPERLY?**

It was just a question. The point I am trying to make is that our children need to know what friendship is before they start having friends. They need to know what love is before they go out and start making babies. They need to know the true meaning and context of intimacy, so they do not become abused or an abuser. That is my take. You may or may not agree.

Children do not need to be *hospitalized, neglected* or ostracized, as these experiences, as you can imagine, would obviously have a detrimental effect on their ability to form and maintain emotionally significant relationships.

Many people do not know **TRUE LOVE** which is the **DIVINE**. The world is living proof of this statement. Please correct me if I am wrong.

Whose children are running around at present. Is it the **GOD'S** or the **DEVIL'S**? What does the future bring for our beloved(s)?

(4)   ESTEEM – (Low Esteem, High Esteem)

We need to teach our children **self–mastery**. If our children have a purpose, are well-disciplined and have full knowledge of themselves and their roots, I think that they can't go wrong. With **GOOD SELF-ESTEEM,** they will be going somewhere as they have direction and are equipped with patience and knowledge to see things through. If our children have no **PURPOSE,** no **KNOWLEDGE OF SELF** or no **MORALS,** how can **WE** expect them to **SUCCEED** in this **LIFE?**

Let's make this not the case.
We need to **ALL** think to **OURSELVES:** have we **EQUIPPED** our children for this **LIFE?**

(5)   SELF ACTUALISATION – (Mate Acquisition, Parenting, Utilising Abilities, Utilising Talents, Pursuing a Goal, Seeking Happiness).

"What a man can be, he must be." – Abraham Maslow. [2]

We need to help **OUR CHILDREN** to **BECOME** the **BEST** version of themselves that they can **BE!**

I DO NOT MEAN TO OFFEND IN ANY WAY. IT IS THE WAY I FEEL!

My parents tried their best with me, but I don't feel that they received the support, guidance and skills to even bring a child into the world. I speak for myself, too. I have a 23-year-old daughter whom I have brought into this world, and it was unfair, really. I say

[2] Maslow, A. (1954). Motivation and Personality. New York: Harper.

that now as I have not done the greatest job as a parent myself. I am not afraid to say that.

Why?

Because I am 43 years old, and I am just realizing what life is about. I am not there yet, but I am getting there. I should have been there first before bringing souls into this world. What do you think?

We humans have something inside us which burns away; some are conscious of it, others not. With our children, it burns really bright – if only they knew.

What is it you may ask?

A burning desire to reach our full potential. This is inborn in us humans as Maslow's studies highlight. We need to find ourselves and find what **POWER** we bring to this "**WORLD** table."

CHAPTER 2:

MUSIC

C an I ask you something, please?

Do you have children?

What music do your children listen to?

What effect does this music have on them, **do you know?**

I used to like **RAP** (Rhythm and Poetry) and **Hip-Hop** music when I was younger. I still like some, but music has changed so much, and not for the best. Unfortunately, this is just my own opinion. You may or may not agree.

It is all about tones, frequencies and content. Are you educated in these affairs?

I am slowly becoming aware.

I was listening to an old lecture from Professor Griff today, you know, the gentleman from the Public Enemy rap band back in the day? He made it about 9 years ago, but the content is still relevant today.

I will leave the link below for you. You should watch it if you get a chance:

https://www.youtube.com/watch?v=OeREN_rwnVA

He really did get me thinking. You see, Professor Griff has been in the music business since I was a child, and he has a vast wealth of knowledge on this subject area. He has even been persecuted over the years by the establishment and media for constantly speaking the **TRUTH**. If you don't believe me, check it out for yourself.

Griff starts off by referring to the works of Bill Cooper, whose real name is Milton William Cooper, a former United States Naval Intelligence Briefing Team member. He was renowned for revealing top secret information that had been hidden from the public eye by the government and the establishment. I remember rapper Prodigy from Mobb Deep used to speak about Bill often.

Prodigy and Bill both died under mysterious circumstances. Both men were well known and respected for speaking the **TRUTH** about things which **WE,** the **PUBLIC,** may have been unaware of. They have not been the only ones and probably will not be the last.

We all know that **MEDIA** is **BIG BUSINESS**. We should also know that it can be manipulated as a **TOOL** used to **CONTROL** or **PROGRAM** people, countries and nations.

What we need to realize as a parent is that music is nature, music is science. When you break music down, it is all about tones and frequencies, which directly relate to us. The planet is made up of tones and frequencies, as are we.

When you read into quantum physics, you will notice that sound waves bounce and come back off themselves. Similarly, the human body is vibrating sound, and all our thought patterns are sound in order to become energy and emotions.

Therefore, we should make sure that our **CHILDREN** are not **EXPOSED** to **HARMFUL MUSIC** which may **REPROGRAM** their subconscious **MIND!** When you look into things this way, you can see how things really are if you are ready **NOT** to **IGNORE** the **FACTS**.

In Bill Cooper's book "Behold a Pale Horse," he speaks about the American public:

"*DIVERSION IS THE PRIMARY STRATEGY;* the simplest method for securing silent weapons and gaining is by keeping the public undisciplined and ignorant of basic system principles while keeping them confused."

Bill also states that this is the reason for reality TV shows being produced, as these shows distract and confuse people. They confuse people about politics, gender, sexuality and their role in society. The media keeps the general adult population's attention diverted away from real social issues and replaced by matters of no real importance. Schools are keeping children ignorant of real mathematics, real economics, real law and real history. Entertainment is kept below the sixth-grade level. This is not very nice, is it?

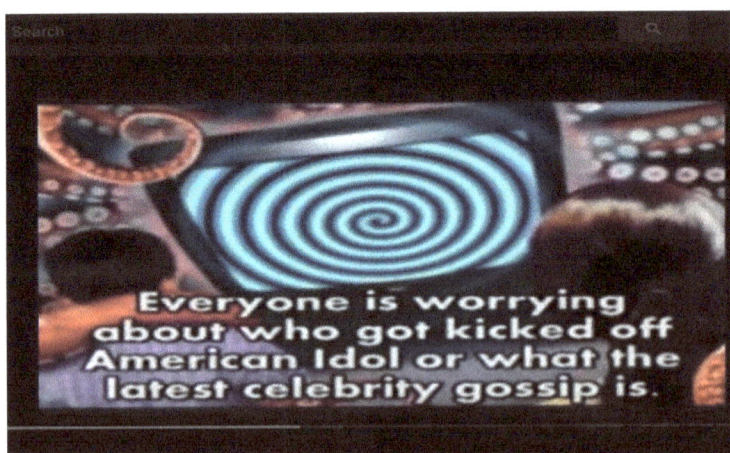

Source: [3]

Griff supports this statement in his video. He refers to several examples. He is a man that **KNOWS**; he has

[3] https://www.youtube.com/watch?v=OeREN_rwnVA accessed Dec 29[th,] 2018 @ 00:02

both inside and outside knowledge of the industry. He states that songs like "Laffy Taffy," are designed to hit our lower chakra, which vibrates negative energy and activates our pituitary gland that releases our hormones. He also points out that we now have "GROWN ASS MEN, MAKING SONGS FOR 12 OR 13-YEAR-OLDS," such as the likes of Jay-Z. So, **WE** are kept busy working, giving us no **TIME** to **THINK**. I think that is the **PLAN**.

John Coleman, a former British intelligence agent, another **BRAVE** "whistle-blower" himself, who had access to sources the rest of us cannot reach, published this information in a book called "The Tavistock Institute of Human Relations: Shaping the Morals, Spiritual, Culture and Economic Decline of the United States." He also authored a book called "The Conspirators' Hierarchy: The Committee of 300," which addresses how an international council organizes *politics, commerce, banking, media and the military* for centralized global efforts.

It is the committee 300 who decide what the trends are going to be: if the rappers will be wearing saggy pants or if the punks will have spikey hair. Can you see where I am coming from?

Can you not **SEE** what's happening out there? Rihanna dyes her hair red and before you know it, a great chunk of the female population follows suit. I have witnessed it with my own eyes, all this **brainwashing, distractions, social engineering, predicted programming** and

manipulation. This is not even half of the issues that **WE** are faced with as **MEDIA CONSUMERS**.

We need to be careful what music is fed to our children and also ourselves, as it is our **SOULS** which are at stake. I know I sound like the old "mumbly grumbly," but it is true what I say. If you don't believe me, check it out for yourself.

I am no longer interested in mainstream music as it doesn't make sense, as you can see.

My favorite artists are gone, (**prematurely,** I must add), most under mysterious circumstances.

(Call me a conspiracy nut if you like, but this is all too crazy for me. What do you feel?)

- Bob Marley - gone
- Eazy-E - gone
- Jam Master Jay – gone
- Lil Snupe - gone
- Lisa "Left Eye" Lopes – gone
- Michael Jackson – gone
- Nate Dogg - gone
- Notorious B.I.G. – gone
- Ol' Dirty Bastard - gone
- Pimp C - gone
- Prince – gone

- Tupac – gone

It appears that they were either "**speaking out,**" not doing what they were paid for, not respecting their **contracts** or delivering the wrong messages, just kidding.

It doesn't really make sense, or does it?

Check out the following extract that I read today:

"The premature death of dozens of icons and pop stars over the past decades has left the world bereft of natural talent, allowing the music and entertainment industry to promote manufactured bands, like Busted or Blue! Plane crashes are a common cause of death for the rich and famous, many more, like Marilyn Monroe or Brian Jones, have died in **mysterious** circumstances."

"While some celebrity deaths may be self-inflicted, such as Sid Vicious, who died from a drug overdose, aged twenty-one, the majority are suspicious. Personalities or performers with originality and ingenuity are martyrs of '**Operation Mockingbird**' to be **replaced** by mediocre, compliant **clones**. But the **NWO** can't kill music; true talent is irrepressible, and this is so **scary and unreal**... it's just horrific...what are **your thoughts?**" [4]

I am not sure if this is true or not, but it most definitely gets you thinking.

Professor Griff speaks about "**Operation Paperclip**" during his preoccupation in the CIA. The programme involved the development of techniques of behavior control, such as brainwashing, covert medical and psychic experimentation on unwitting subjects including religious sects, ethnic minorities, prisoners, mental patients, soldiers and the terminally ill. Who knows? Is this really going on right in front of our noses?

Please check this out:

"The Impact of Song Lyrics on Our Children: What You Need to Know

We've heard that graphically violent computer games and cartoons can affect behavior, causing children to become more violent. But most parents are completely unaware of the impact of sexualized lyrics in popular music on teenagers. How would they know it's a problem when they don't even know what their children are listening to?

---

[4] https://warningilluminati.wordpress.com/the-illuminati-assassination-list/ accessed Dec 29[th,] 2018 @ 18:06

Technology has made it easy to listen to music in a crowded room without disturbing anyone. Devices such as iPods and MP4 players have made music more portable and lightweight earphones afford the listener an amazing degree of privacy.

So, where does that leave us as parents?

Parents don't know that sexualized song lyrics are a growing trend. They never hear their children's music because the children are using earphones. And it doesn't occur to parents that this is something they need to know about or research. After all, what could be bad about music? What could be more universal than teenage attraction to popular music?

So, what is it doing to them, to our children, hearing all those sexed-up lyrics?

Well, for one thing, it's giving them the wrong impression about their peers' sexual behavior. Teens tend to think their friends are engaging in more sexual activity than they actually are. Experts have found a connection between these overblown perceptions and entertainment media such as music, games, and movies.

The fact that teens believe their peers are more sexually advanced than they actually are, leads teens to challenge themselves to increase their sexual activity to play "catch-up." They may worry they aren't grown up enough or cool enough because they aren't doing what they think their friends are doing. Meanwhile, adolescents are at risk of contracting _sexually transmitted diseases_ such as genital herpes, for instance. They are also at risk of teenage pregnancy."[5]

Now check out this next article. It is another one that gets you **THINKING!**

"BEYONCÈ AND JAY–Z: THE RUMOR NOBODY IS TALKING ABOUT"

"And the winner is.... Our very own Brittaneè Perkins!"

---

[5] https://www.kars4kids.org/blog/the-impact-of-song-lyrics-on-our-children-what-you-need-to-know/ accessed Dec 30th, 2018 @ 06:18

"With utter shock on my face, I shrill in excitement and accept my prize! I was just announced as the winner of 2 tickets to the Jay-Z and Beyoncé On the Run Tour!

But after the initial excitement wears off, reality sets in. I had just won tickets to see musicians that I denounced after getting **SAVED** 8 months ago. I am not a Beyoncé hater; I have been a Beyoncé FANATIC since the 4th grade, and I still have the destiny's child dolls, concert ticket stubs, and DVD's to prove it. But her last album was not the Bey I grew up loving. I remember the days when Bey was sexy, but not sexually explicit. She did not curse on records and wasn't so brazen. So, I decided to stop listening to her and Jay-Z's music because I do not believe it, in any way, glorifies God. (clarification: I won the tickets through an employee sweepstakes that my job held for those who participated in volunteer efforts outside of work- I did not call a radio station or go out of my way to get them).

I instantly felt convicted. I would never **pay** to see Beyoncé and Jay-Z on this tour (it's raunchy and way too expensive for my blood). But would I be strong enough to take a stand for Christ even if the tickets were free? I felt like a hypocrite for even considering going.

Anyway, after much prayer, consideration, and conversation with my parents and Pastor, I decided to go. Attending a Beyoncè concert won't send you to hell, just like attending a Kirk Franklin concert won't get you into heaven. 'It's harmless entertainment,' I said to myself."

"How bad could it be?"

3rd August 2014: Rose Bowl Stadium

Me and my bestie before the show

"From the moment Jay-Z and Beyoncé hit the stage, something felt off in my spirit. I knew I didn't belong there, and I felt heavy and out of place. Instead of cheering and singing along to the songs I once loved, I literally began taking notes. Let me be clear: this is not some 'Illuminati conspiracy' post created to discuss secret occult symbols used by a secular artist. I won't even go into the deep stuff. This is much more simple—which makes it even worse. This concert had a 42 song setlist, so I also won't attempt to cover every detail. These were my personal notes on 12 of the most blatant things that stood out to me.

During the show's opening song 'Bonnie and Clyde,' they come out with a **HUGE** cross in the back of them. **'All I need in this life of sin is me and my girlfriend.'** Actually, all you need in this life of sin is Jesus and a repentant heart! Your girlfriend can't save you on judgment day, and I can't believe how long it took me to realize the subtle message they are spreading with this catchy song. The unnecessary huge cross combined with lyrics mentioning sin threw me off. Anybody who knows what happened on the cross and has accepted Jesus as their Savior should have more respect for it.

2. Beyoncé is now wearing a thong and provocatively dancing for the crowd. I understand that she is an 'entertainer,' but where does a wife and mother of a little girl draw the line? I was even more appalled that her husband was okay with this. **Beyoncé has the talent, she doesn't have to come out naked to sell records.**

3. Jay-Z says, **'I had to get off the boat, so I could walk on water.'** Ummm, like the miracle Jesus performed? So now you perform miracles like Jesus? Or are you Peter? Either way, for someone who does not identify as a believer, he sure does use a ton of biblical references. Interesting.

4. Jay-Z says, 'Shout out all the weed smokers,' and repeatedly calls his wife and mother of his child a 'bad b***h,' as she nods and sings along in agreement. A bad b***h is a dog that misbehaves, not your wife and the mother of your daughter.

5. Beyoncé starts singing **'Who run the World? Girls.'** The bible tells us it is Satan, not girls who run the world. John 12:31 'The time for judging this world has come, when Satan, the ruler of this world, will be cast out.' Then, I notice Beyoncé singing a phrase, almost as if she is casting a spell. **'My persuasion can build a**

nation, endless power, a love you can devour, you'll do anything for me.' I instantly think of 1 Peter 5:8 'Stay alert! Watch out for your great enemy, the devil. He prowls around like a roaring lion, looking for someone to devour.' This song sets the tone for the rest of the concert, as everyone began to follow along as if they were hypnotized.

6. 'The hypnosis' is immediately followed by a song in which Beyoncé repeatedly sings **'Bow Down b****es'** over and over again. And please don't try to tell me 'Flawless' is a women's empowerment anthem. In the same song she uses to convey the feminist message that women are tearing each other down and using their looks to compete for a man's attention, she is telling me to 'bow down' to her while she opens her legs and shakes her bum in

front of thousands of men. By the way, I don't care what Beyonce says, WE ARE NOT FLAWLESS. In fact, we are the opposite and need God's grace and mercy because we really deserve his wrath.

Did I mention Beyoncé says 'God Damn' 14 times?

7. Next, Jay-Z has water in the background, which gives the appearance he is walking on water. At times, the screen shows the water splitting like the Red Sea. Yet another biblical reference. Not surprised since he already thinks he is God. **'Hova' is definitely short for Jehovah.**

8. **Crosses.** So many crosses. Burning crosses. Crosses surrounded by fire. Big red crosses. I saw so

many that I lost count. And these crosses are constantly being displayed while the artists sing lyrics about pride, vanity, sex, getting drunk, cheating, and self-glorification.

9. It's a rap concert, so I expected some cursing. But the cursing in this concert was crazy! I am not talking a few darns and s*words. I'm talking 22 F*bombs and 17 Mf'*rs. Oh, let me clarify, they came from Beyoncé, not Jay-Z. At times I felt I was watching Rihanna instead of Mrs. Carter. If you want to call yourself a Queen, then you need to speak like one.

10. The words **'Lucifer, Dawn of the Morning,'** randomly blares from the speakers. Jay-Z doesn't even perform this song. I guess they just wanted to say Lucifer to the crowd to remind us who this was all about.

11. Jay-Z performs 'No Church in the Wild,' a song that boasts lyrics like, 'What's a king to a God, what's a God to a non-believer?' Jay-Z then says, 'Jesus was a carpenter, Yeezus laid the beat, Hova flow the Holy Ghost get the f*** up out ya seats.' He then goes on to say, 'We gotta thank God for letting us live out our dream!' Huh? You're 'Thanking God' on the same track in which your chorus includes 'What's a God to a non-believer?' Who is the God that you are thanking?

12. Instead of 'J+B,' I notice it keeps showing 'J†B.' A cross is used instead of a plus sign.

These were just a few of the many things I noticed during the show. As a Christian, it rightfully made me feel very uncomfortable, and I would question my salvation if it didn't. Beyoncé can do whatever she wants to, but she needs to mindful that she has boldly presented herself to the world as a Christian. A tree is identified by its fruit. Everyone is talking about how this concert sold 100 million tickets, and how the Carters may be headed to divorce court but breezing over the message of this tour. We have to be aware of what we are feeding our spirits, and I personally refuse to let a catchy hook and dope beat lead me to hell.

Ephesians 6:12 'For we wrestle not against flesh and blood, but against principalities, against powers, against the rulers of the darkness of this world, against spiritual wickedness in high places.' One time for the nation, ~Britt" [6]

I am not religious in any way, shape or form, but I can relate to some of the things that Britt is speaking about. We might know what is going on, **BUT DO OUR CHILDREN?** It is not just Jay-Z and Beyoncé. All this **ENTERTAINMENT** "malarkey" is commonplace amongst **MOST** popular music. **WE** just need to be aware of what **MESSAGE** is being **TRANSMITTED** to **OUR CHILDREN** and **OURSELVES**.

There's just one more thing that I would like to finish off with. Have you ever heard of backmasking?

What is backmasking, you ask?

"Top 10 Famous Cases of Backmasking

Andrew C. 28th August 2011

Backmasking is the process of reversing an audio signal and placing it in something meant to be played forwards. When played normally the

[6] http://savedsingleme.com/beyonce-and-jay-z-the-rumor-nobody-is-talking-about/ accessed Dec 30[th,] 2018 @ 06:54

message will sound like gibberish, however, when the song is played in reverse the original message can be heard. Some of the first instances of reversed audio were the result of The Beatles' experimentation during the recording of Revolver. Since then, backmasked messages have turned up in all kinds of music with messages ranging from humorous to satanic. Today, reversing audio is a popular way to censor explicit words for radio. Here is a list of 10 famous instances of backmasking.

(10) The Mars Volta - Eunuch Provocateur

http://www.youtube.com/watch?v=W2a-5dHLico

The Mars Volta is a prog-rock band known for cryptic lyrics and messages. One instance that had fans buzzing was on the track 'Eunuch Provocateur' on their EP Tremulant. At 5:30, the track transforms into echoing drums with an eerie guitar. A voice can be heard, but none of the words can be made out. Fans found that when played in reverse the gibberish could be heard as 'The Itsy Bitsy Spider.' The band used an old record that contained children's songs for the samples. Also, in the track, the phrase 'Did mommy or daddy ever have to spank you?' can be heard when reversed.

(9) Missy Elliot – Work It

http://www.youtube.com/watch?v=kK_OifqZUwc

Missy Elliot used backmasking for aesthetic purposes on her track 'Work It' from her album Under Construction. The chorus of the track is 'Is it worth it, let me work it, I put my thing down flip it and reverse it' followed by backwards gibberish. When the gibberish is played in reverse, it says 'I put my thing down flip it and reverse it.' Missy sampled the previous line of the chorus and reversed it. In the same song at around 2:08 Missy says 'Listen up close while I take you backwards' followed by the reversed message 'Watch the way Missy like to take it backwards.'

(8) Weird Al Yankovic – I Remember Larry

In the late 80s and early 90s, parents and special interest groups began accusing artists of using backmasking to hide disturbing and even satanic messages. These accusations resulted in court cases over high profile artists. Weird Al poked fun at the issue and hid a humorous message about those searching for hidden messages on the track 'I Remember Larry' off his album, Bad Hair Day. In the bridge of the song at around 3:14, Al's voice can be heard speaking nonsense. When reversed one can hear 'Wow, you must have an awful lot of free time on your hands.'

(7) Queen - Another One Bites the Dust

In the early 1980's, Queen was accused of hiding a reversed message in their song 'Another One Bites the Dust.' Christian evangelists claimed that when played in reverse the lyrics 'Another one bites the dust' becomes 'It's fun to smoke marijuana.' Some believed since the song had other strange effects on it, it was possible the band had purposely used backmasking to hide the pro-marijuana message. A spokesperson for Hollywood Records denied that the song contained a hidden message. The message is widely considered to be unintended. Many cite this song as an example of phonetic reversal, where a word when reversed, sounds like another word.

(6) Jay-Z - Lucifer

Jay-Z is a popular rapper who is often tied to many conspiracy theories. Some popular theories propose that he is satanic and is linked to the Illuminati and freemasons. While the theories about him are far-fetched, believers of these theories thought they found proof when the song 'Lucifer 9' was reversed. Gibberish played normally; this was the message '666 murder murder Jesus 666' when played backwards. What many people don't know is the track 'Lucifer 9' was actually from Danger mouse's The Grey Album. The Grey Album was a mashup of The Beatles (White Album) and Jay-Z's the Black Album. Danger mouse chopped up Jay-Z acapellas and created the message over The Beatles 'Revolution 9.'

(5) Pink Floyd - Empty Spaces

Pink Floyd used backmasking to hide a message on their song 'Empty Spaces' from the album The Wall. Gibberish is heard when listening to the song normally. When played in reverse a secret message is found:

'Hello, Luka... Congratulations. You have just discovered the secret message. Please send your answer to Old Pink, care of the Funny Farm, Chalfont...
- Roger! Carolyn's on the phone!
- Okay.'

The message is supposedly Roger Waters addressing people who look for hidden messages. Waters congratulates them and asks them to send a response to 'Old Pink' at the 'Funny Farm.' Before Waters can give the full address, he is notified by someone that his wife, Carolyn, is on the phone. Many think 'Old Pink' is a reference to former member Syd Barrett who had mental problems and was in a psychiatric hospital ('Funny Farm').

(4) The Beatles - I'm So Tired

The Beatles self-titled 1968 album (White Album) was thoroughly searched for clues about Paul's death rumours (see #2) by fans. One of the most noticeable pieces of supposed evidence was a backmasked message at the end of 'I'm So Tired.' At the very end of the song, as the music is fading out, John Lennon can be heard speaking incomprehensibly. When played in reverse, some hear the words 'Paul is a dead man, miss him, miss him, miss him.' While many saw this as evidence of Paul's death the rumour was denied by the band. Paul McCartney also denies the rumours of his death.

(3) Judas Priest - Better by You, Better than Me

In 1990, Judas Priest was involved in a court case which alleged subliminal messages in their song 'Better by You, better than Me' led to the suicide, and attempted suicide, of two men in 1985. Allegedly, Raymond Belknap and James Vance drank beer and smoked marijuana for several hours while listening to Judas Priest. They then went to a church playground, where Belknap shot himself under the chin with a 12-gauge shotgun, dying instantly. Vance then tried to do the same. However, the gun slipped as he fired, blowing away the lower half of his face. He later told a reporter of a suicide pact he made with Belknap, 'We had been programmed. I knew I was going to do it. I was afraid. I didn't want to die. It's just as if I had no choice.' He slipped into a coma three years later and died. The men's parents filed a civil action which alleged that, when played backwards, the Judas Priest track encouraged listeners to commit suicide and 'Do it.' The suit was dismissed.
*Note: I can't hear anything that sounds like 'Do it.'

(2) The Beatles - Revolution 9

The Beatles (White Album) contained an avant-garde track titled 'Revolution 9.' The track contained lots of effects and noise and was noteworthy for how odd it was. In 1969, as the rumours of Paul McCartney's death were spreading, Revolution 9 became an important piece of evidence to those claiming Paul was dead. A caller to a Detroit Radio Show explained possible evidence of Paul's death and convinced disc jockey Russ Gibb to play Revolution 9 in reverse. The repeated phrase 'number nine' became 'turn me on dead man' when played backwards. Listeners called into the phone lines to voice their opinions, which further spread the rumours. When played in reverse many claims to hear other clues such as the sound of a car crash and someone screaming 'Let me out.'

Led Zeppelin - Stairway to Heaven

In January 1982, Paul Crouch accused many rock artists of hiding messages in their songs through backmasking. One example he pointed out was the Led Zeppelin song 'Stairway to Heaven.'

When played normally one hears:
'If there's a bustle in your hedgerow, don't be alarmed now
It's just a spring clean for the May queen
Yes, there are two paths you can go by, but in the long run

There's still time to change the road you're on.'
When played in reverse Crouch said a satanic
message could be heard:
'Oh here's to my sweet Satan.
The one whose little path would make me sad,
whose power is Satan.
He will give those with him 666.
There was a little tool shed where he made us
suffer, sad Satan.'

The band ignored these claims; however, Swan Song
Records issued a statement saying, 'Our turntables
only play in one direction...forwards.' The alleged
satanic message has become, arguably, the most
famous instance of backmasking, adding to the
mystery and legacy of Led Zeppelin. Many,
however, say it's merely a coincidence and is simply
another case of phonetic reversal." [7]

Check the link on footnote[8] if you get a chance; it
shows a list of many, many backmasked **messages**
which have been inserted in the music that we
consume. I don't know if there is any truth in any of
this apart from what we can plainly see, but I really

---

[7] http://listverse.com/2011/08/28/top-10-famous-cases-of-backmasking/ accessed Dec 30[th,] 2018 @ 07:03

[8] Unknown

felt the need to share it with you. This information could, maybe, help improve the world and its **GOLDEN ONES**. Who knows?

Can you please do me a favor?

Look up the word incantation.

This appears to be rife in the music industry, superficially being used to place spells upon people (with a hidden agenda in mind). If you don't believe me, please check it out for yourself.

Artists play tricks with words, music and tones. They do this by a little trick on words within the music, which is written in "witch language." They do this because as long as the artists can get the person to say the words of the song, not knowing what they're saying, they would, in fact, be putting a spell on themselves, surely?

What do you think? Maybe we are being influenced and attacked by the radio waves also? I think it depends upon the tones and frequencies, who **knows?**

Do you?

I feel it is best that we _DO NOT_ feed our CHILDRENs' minds, bodies and souls to the wolves, WHAT DO YOU THINK?

CHAPTER 3:

SWEETS

Are sweets good for children?

"'Sweets are good for children and may stop them getting fat in later life,' reported by **The Daily Mail.**

This news story is based on a U.S. study that assessed the diet of more than 11,000 children and adolescents over 24 hours. Researchers looked at how their confectionery consumption related to their total energy consumption, body fat and other measures of heart health, such as blood pressure and blood fats. Those who ate sweets or chocolate were found to have higher total energy and added sugar intake but were less likely to be overweight or obese.

The study has numerous limitations which limit the conclusions that can be drawn." [9]

According to The Daily Mail, they are after 24 hours' worth of testing on the children, whereas our NHS is unsure. Strange!

Please check out the next extract that was published 28th October 2014, if you wouldn't mind.

---

[9] https://www.nhs.uk/news/pregnancy-and-child/are-sweets-good-for-kids/ accessed Dec 31st, 2018 @ 21:00

Elizabeth Narins has put together quite a good little report, please see overleaf:

"9 Halloween Candies You Should Never Eat

And smarter ways to satisfy your cravings.

A little bit of candy isn't going to kill you. But there are smart ways to treat yourself — especially on the holiday that revolves around the sweet stuff. And no matter what goes down this Halloween, avoid the candies that could spook your body well after your costume comes off, according to registered dietitian _Keri Glassman_, cosmetic dentist _Dr. Marc Lowenberg_, and the Environmental Working Group's _Food Scores_:

1. Gummies made with sticky glucose syrup, gummy candies (like Gummy Bears, Sour Patch Kids, and Jelly Beans) can easily get wedged in the pits and grooves of your teeth. 'It's nearly impossible for saliva to wash that away,' Dr. Lowenberg says. And when sugar hangs around in your mouth, the decay-causing bacteria go to town on your teeth, which can lead to cavities.

Instead, go for DIY candy corn snack mix. The ultimate Halloween candies aren't good for you — but compared to gummies, they're slightly less sticky. Because calories and sugar do add up, mix some candy corn with a few cups of low-calorie air-popped popcorn. You'll get a larger, more satisfying snack that's still festive.

Skittles, inside their little candy shells, Skittles are almost as sticky as gummy candies, so they can make a real mess of your teeth. Besides that, Skittles aren't much more than artificial colors and processed sugar. If you consume large quantities (which is bound to happen on Halloween), your body could end up storing it as fat, Glassman says.

Instead, go for: Fruit leather with no added sugar, which delivers fruity flavors without the yucky stuff. (Or, if you're all like, 'That totally doesn't count!' opt for Nerds. They're no less processed, but they are at least less sticky than Skittles, so they'll be easier on your teeth.)

3. Raisinettes Chocolate-covered fruit may sound healthy. The thing is, when your dry fruit, you end up with a sticky ball of sugar that's not a whole lot healthier than straight-up candy.

Instead, go for dark chocolate. No one craves raisins — so you might as well go for the good stuff, straight up. Pure chocolate is designed to melt when it comes in contact with high temperatures in your mouth, so it won't really stick to your teeth. And while dark chocolate is a far cry from kale, it's less processed than milk chocolate. It is a good source of iron and fiber and has been linked to some _surprising health benefits_.

4. Snickers The caramel in these candy bars can spell trouble for your teeth.

Instead, go for Peanut M&Ms or a Mr. Goodbar. They will satisfy your craving for nuts and chocolate without caramel hanging around in your mouth. Plus, the peanuts contain healthy fats and protein, which can help steady your sugar high.

5. Twix These crunchy candies also contain caramel, which is no-go if you'd like to keep your teeth intact.

Instead, go for Kit-Kats. They're not healthy by any means, but the chocolate-covered biscuits should hit the spot without the stickiness.

6. Caramel Apple Lollipops 'Lollipops and other hard candy are among the worst candies to consume because they take the longest to dissolve,' Dr. Lowenberg says. 'The longer the candy remains on your teeth, the longer the bacteria that causes cavities start to decay the teeth.' This treat, in particular, is made with tons of random synthetic ingredients and not a bit of apple.

Instead, go for Dum Dums. Yes, they're lollipops. But they're free of sticky caramel, and they're super tiny, so they will be finished and out of your mouth before you know. it.

7. Butterfingers, they basically glue themselves to your teeth, but that's not the worst of it: Butterfingers contain manmade trans fats, ingredients derived from genetically engineered crops, and synthetic food dyes, according to data from the Environmental Working Group. Plus, they're not even made from real chocolate — just 'compound chocolate,' a cheap way to coat candy, Glassman says.

Instead, go for Hershey's Milk Chocolate Nuggets or Kisses with Almonds for legitimate chocolate, a little crunch, and some protein and fiber.

8. Reeses Peanut Butter Cups. Peanut butter and chocolate can be paired to make a healthy-enough treat — but this isn't it. The filling isn't made from pure peanut butter, but from emulsifiers and preservatives and loads of sugar, Glassman says. (Unfortunately, the cute pumpkin-shaped cups are no better.)

Instead, go for Justin's Dark Chocolate Peanut Butter Cups. Dark chocolate generally contains more antioxidants, fiber, and iron, and less sugar than milk chocolate. This particular treat is made from natural ingredients produced without synthetic pesticides and genetic engineering.

9. Starbursts. Don't let the fruit flavors fool you. These chewy squares are made primarily of corn syrup and sugar and both ingredients are derived from genetically engineered crops. Figure in the synthetic food dyes and trans fats, and you've got a product that's closer to Frankenstein than actual food.

Instead, go for Haribo. They're not good for your teeth (see No. 1 above), but they are better for your body than Starbursts. They contain less sugar by weight and none of the manmade fats known to mess with your health. Just brush and floss extra well after you eat them." [10]

In most places that I have researched, I have found that is it okay to eat sweets as long as we do not eat too much. That does seem to be the general consensus.

I may be "going against the grain here." I could be totally wrong, but I disagree. I am going to sound very strange now, but I feel that sweets should not even be on the Plan-**E.T.**

We tend to be moving away from fruits and vegetables and moving towards synthetic **NICE-TASTING** foods like sweets and chocolates.

What about the mineral content and nutritional value? Is it up to human consumption standards? Is it safe and fit for us?

How have all the sweets got through FDA testing?

Despite whatever is being said, I am still not convinced.

Most sweets have a lot of sugar which we all know is **VERY BAD.**

------

[10] https://www.cosmopolitan.com/food-cocktails/advice/ a32560/halloween-candies-you-should-never-eat/ accessed Dec 31th, 2018 @ 21:51

Some have glucose which could cause **TOOTH DECAY**.

Others have artificial coloring and preservatives.

Some contain gelatine which comes from collagen obtained from animal body parts.

Some have syrup and dairy products which we all should know is not great.

I forgot to mention the **GMOs** (Genetically Modified).

Please correct me if I am wrong in any of this. It is just my personal view which I felt like sharing with you. I am no expert.

I wish I was not introduced to sweets in the first place. I don't really eat them often but regret it every time. I think I must suffer from temporary relapse or maybe I need to strengthen my mind or move away from all the **negative distractions**. Who knows?

My moral on this is that I wouldn't give to my children anything that would be detrimental to their well-being in any way, shape or form. If I am not 100% sure about something, I would never give it to my children. I have experienced a lot in this life which I wish I had never encountered.

In the past, I have been indoctrinated into many things by family, friends and acquaintances (I am not afraid to admit), but now I know **BETTER**.

NOW, if I am not sure, I like to check and research things properly, but really, I am not so sure on the sweet's ideology. Each to their own, I guess.

CHAPTER 4:

MINERALS &

VACCINATIONS

Have you ever looked at the anatomy of the human body?

I am sure you have; we must have all learned about it at school.

Did you know that the human body is made up of 102 minerals?

THE 103 MINERALS THAT MAKE UP THE HUMAN BODY

As you can see there are 103 minerals that make up the human body. Oxygen was not included in Dr Sebi's 102 minerals due to the fact that we do not take in oxygen through food intake, but I added it as oxygen is the most important element for most types of life on this planet. There is around 61% oxygen amount in the human body which is chiefly obtained by liquefying air.
Oxygen as we know it is the most common element on the surface of the Earth occurring as oxygen gas in water and oxide minerals or in combination with elements in silicates, phosphates, sulphates, etc. [11]

[11] https://mineralseducationcoalition.org/elements/oxygen/ accessed 25th January 2020 @ 18:24

To be fully nourished, we **HUMANS** have to consume food which would give us these minerals. Did you know that?

Have you noticed anything else?

Protein is nowhere to be found on this list. Why is that?

You see, the human body is made up of the <u>SAME</u> basic minerals and elements that are our natural resources. We are a part of nature, and that's what we must all realize.

"The aforementioned article, *'A glaring example of how false science holds the truth in unrighteousness,'* includes a table entitled, 'Human Body Composition.' The table plainly shows that man is composed of the dust of the earth." [12]

Please check out the link below to see the report and table:

http://www.jesus-is-lord.com/glaring.htm

Dr. Sebi bought this to our attention many years ago. The human body is a very complex "entity." Check out the following extract from my good brother Aqiyl Aniys, who is doing a great job supporting the legacy of good old Dr.

---

[12] http://www.jesus-is-lord.com/glaring.htm accessed Dec 31th, 2018 @ 06:54

Sebi, who, unfortunately, died prematurely under suspicious and mysterious circumstances.

Please see the extract:

"The methodology revolves around the 102 minerals that the body is made up of and the minerals need to be replenished through consuming alkaline plant food Dr. Sebi says the body is made up of.

A mineral must be a naturally occurring 'element' or 'chemical compound' formed by geological processes (formation of the earth) and not by biological processes (sea shells). Understanding this concept is important in understanding what Dr. Sebi meant by the term 'mineral.' There are over 5000 known naturally occurring compound minerals.

Since there are so many naturally occurring 'compound minerals' and Dr. Sebi speaks of 102 minerals making up the body then it would appear he was referring to the elements and not the compounds. Elements are the individual parts of a compound. Iron, phosphorous, and oxygen are individual elements that make up iron phosphate.

An agreed-upon criteria for something to be a mineral is it needs to be a solid at room temperature. This is where things can become a little tricky using the term 'mineral.' Elements like oxygen, hydrogen, and nitrogen are gases at room temperature and are elements that are part of the air we breathe.

102 Minerals

It is a bit tricky trying isolate which 102 minerals Dr. Sebi referred to because it appears, he used the concepts of 'elements,' 'minerals,' and 'compounds minerals' interchangeably. It does appear when he especially spoke about the 102 minerals the body is made of, he was referring to elements or single minerals.

An element is an atom made up of a certain number of protons. Every time a proton is added to an atom a new element is formed. For example, hydrogen has 1 proton, carbon has 6 protons, nitrogen has 7 protons, and oxygen has 8 protons.

To support the idea that Dr. Sebi referred to a single element when he spoke about 102 minerals, I looked at the nutrient breakdown of food. Mineral breakdowns are provided for many foods and the mineral content always consists of elements like magnesium, phosphorous, copper, iron, calcium, etc.

There are currently 118 elements listed on the periodic table, but not all of them are naturally occurring they are created in a lab. Only elements 1–92 are naturally occurring elements except for 43 – Technetium (Tc) and 61 – Promethium (Pm). 43 and 61 have a short half–life which is why they are not found naturally on earth. 43 has been detected in stars. All elements past 92 -uranium haven't been found on earth and are produced in a lab.

http://www.angelo.edu/faculty/kboudrea/periodic/phys ical_natural.htm

This information makes it difficult to identify which 102 'minerals/elements' Dr. Sebi referred to as making up the body. Either Dr. Sebi was referring to the first 102 elements on the Periodic Table, or he was referring to a combination of elements, single minerals and compound minerals." [13]

You can see the rest of the report and the mineral list on Aqiyl's website which is referenced in the footnotes.

Does it look like everything we were taught is a fallacy or misconception?

Science has got it wrong; I know.

Maybe somebody is lying to us?

Who knows?

Do you know?

It looks like we have been fed wrong knowledge all our life, which I am just coming to realize. The world is definitely not how we perceived it to be.

---

[13] https://www.naturallifeenergy.com/understanding-minerals-in-dr-sebis-african-bio-mineral-balance/ accessed Dec 31th, 2018 @ 07:36

How many minerals are you consuming every day? I know there is a lot of fake food out there: *GMO* foods, *SYNTHETIC* foods. It is not about us. It is about the **CHILDREN, OUR CHILDREN**, the next generation, the **FUTURE**.

Surely, we need to see them, right?

We are actually liquivores, but that is a story for another day.

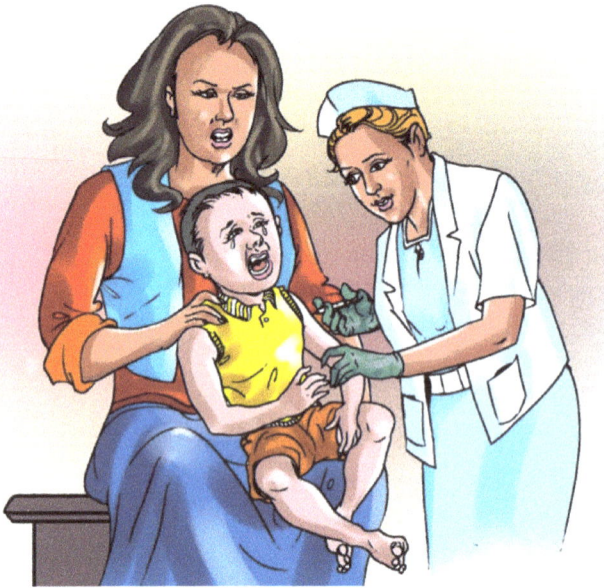

Vaccinations, WHAT A SCARY THING!

I guess Michael Jackson was right when he sang the song "They don't really care about us."

I guess Tupac was right when he sang the song "They don't give a f*ck about us."

Who are **THEY**?

What is going on in this life? We need to know.

How can we teach our children if we don't know ourselves?

What can we teach our children if we don't know ourselves?

Check out an excerpt from my doctor's report:

Mr Adrian Mckenzie					Male		Transferred Out
26/09/2001	HEPATITIS_A	Stage 1	Given			Due 26/03/2002	Claimed 260901 Approved
03/1001	Sister Yvonne Pogue						
19/10/1978	MEASLES	Stage 1	Given	Routine Measure		Due 19/10/1981	
17/08/1978	POLIO	Stage 3	Given	Routine Measure		Due 17/08/1981	
17/08/1978	PERTUSSIS	Stage 3	Given	Routine Measure		Due 17/08/1981	
17/08/1978	TETANUS	Stage 3	Given	Routine Measure		Due 17/08/1981	
17/08/1978	DIPHTHERIA	Stage 3	Given	Routine Measure		Due 17/08/1981	
17/11/1977	POLIO	Stage 2	Given	Routine Measure		Due 15/12/1977	
17/11/1977	PERTUSSIS	Stage 2	Given	Routine Measure		Due 15/12/1977	
17/11/1977	TETANUS	Stage 2	Given	Routine Measure		Due 15/12/1977	
17/11/1977	DIPHTHERIA	Stage 2	Given	Routine Measure		Due 15/12/1977	
06/10/1977	POLIO	Stage 1	Given	Routine Measure		Due 03/11/1977	
06/10/1977	PERTUSSIS	Stage 1	Given	Routine Measure		Due 03/11/1977	
06/10/1977	TETANUS	Stage 1	Given	Routine Measure		Due 03/11/1977	
06/10/1977	DIPHTHERIA	Stage 1	Given	Routine Measure		Due 03/11/1977	
03/12/1976	BCG	Stage 0	Given	Routine Measure		Due	

Absence of condition
21/06/2007   No known allergies of   Dr A Summary

Total patients for report 1

As you can see, from 1976 – 1978 I was given 15 vaccinations or immunizations.

That was when I was between the ages of one and two (thanks mum and dad).

MCKENZIE, Adrian (Mr)
Date of Birth

TRANSITIONAL PRACTICE
NHS Number

12-May-2017	Administration	Invite for NHS Healthcheck
0-Dec-2014	Scanned document	change of address (30-Dec-2014)
11-Jun-2012	Administration	Imported item
06-Jan-2011	EMIS attachment reference code	SL - flu vac
30-Dec-2010	EMIS attachment reference code	flu invite
22-Dec-2010	EMIS attachment reference code	SL - Flu vac invite
13-Oct-2009	EMIS attachment reference code	SL Flu Vac Invite
23-Apr-2009	EMIS attachment reference code	Registration form

Between 2009 and 2011, I was sent three invites to come and take the flu jab?

Medication
No Current Medication
Allergies
No allergies recorded
alth Status

12-Jan-2012	Ex smoker		
12-Jan-2012	Body mass index	26.3	kg/m2
12-Jan-2012	O/E - weight	72	kg
29-May-2009	Notes summary on computer		
23-Apr-2009	O/E Blood Pressure Reading	118/69	mm Hg
23-Apr-2009	O/E - height	165.5	cm
23-Apr-2009	Alcohol consumption	4	units/week

Immunisations

12-Jan-2011	Influenza vaccination declined	3 letters sent no response
26-Sep-2001	Typhoid vaccination	
26-Sep-2001	1st hepatitis A vaccination	
03-Dec-1976	Tuberculosis (BCG) vaccination	

Family History

| 23-Apr-2009 | FH: Breast cancer | Family Member: Aunt |
| 23-Apr-2009 | FH: Asthma | Family Member: Mother |

It looks like I missed my Tuberculosis (BCG) vaccination on 3rd December 1976.

You can see that I was also invited a further three times for my thyroid, influenza and hepatitis injections.

I feel a bit strange thinking about all this: the thought of strangers sticking pins and needles in me, injecting me, taking my blood.

But I suppose it is all for the good of society and me? Thanks, mum and dad?

But is it?

Vaccination	HepB	DTP	Hib	IPV	RV	PCV13	Flu	MMR	Varicella	HepA
Birth	1st									
1 month	2nd									
2 months		1st	1st	1st	1st	1st				
4 months		2nd	2nd	2nd	2nd	2nd				
6 months		3rd	3rd		3rd	3rd				
12 months	3rd		4th			4th	1or2 doses each year	1st	1st	1st & 2nd
15 months		4th		3rd						6 to 18 month apart
18 months										
24 months										
4 to 6 years		5th		4th				2st	2st	

Vaccination Chart

Please check out the next extract:

"The hepatitis B vaccine is a vaccine that was developed for the prevention of hepatitis B infection. In 1981, the first *hepatitis B vaccine* came into use but was discontinued in 1990 because it was an 'inactivated' vaccine and involved the collection of blood from hepatitis B virus-infected (HBsAg-positive) donors.

However, despite the introduction of a 'safer' vaccine in 1986, adverse reactions continued to mount. In 1996, the U.S. alone reported that there had been _872 serious adverse_ events in children under the age of fourteen who had received the hepatitis B vaccine. Out of these, 48 children were said to have died. When you compare these figures to the lower figure of 279 children under the age of fourteen years who actually contracted the hepatitis B infection in the same year, one has to consider whether the vaccine was proving to be more dangerous than the threat of contracting the actual disease.

According to _Dr. Gregory Damato_, a total of 24,775 adverse reactions were reported to the Vaccine Adverse Events Reporting System (VAERS) between 1990 and 1999. These included 439 deaths and 9,673 emergency room visits. There were also reports of arthritis, skin disorders, compromised immunity, autoimmune disease, neurological damage, vision loss and rare eye disorders, such as optic neuritis and epitheliopathy, blood disorders, diabetes, damage to liver and kidneys, severe vomiting, and diarrhea. It is important at this stage to remind ourselves that VAERS is a U.S. based system only, therefore the true number of adverse reactions is not known.

Currently, in the U.S. the hepatitis B vaccine is given to a baby at birth, which many see as unwise unless the baby is known to be at risk from the virus.

Dangerous Ingredients

The current vaccine is cultivated in yeast, which, according to _BioPharm International_, is because:

Yeasts are distinguished by a growing track record as expression platforms for the production of pharmaceuticals. Commercially available, yeast-derived, recombinant pharmaceuticals include insulin, the anti-coagulant hirudin, interferon-alpha-2a, and various vaccines against the hepatitis B virus and papillomavirus infections. The vaccines are produced in either baker's yeast (Saccharomyces cerevisiae), or the methylotrophic species Hansenula polymorpha and Pichia pastoris. In this article, we focus on the production process for hepatitis B vaccines in methylotrophs. Methylotrophs provide highly balanced production of both the membrane and the protein component of a recombinant viral particle.

A brief outlook is given for the development of yeast strains designed for the production of other vaccine candidates.

However, this can cause children with an allergy to yeast to react very severely to the vaccine, which is causing great concern and in accordance, *the Hepatitis B Foundation* has stated:

The vaccine may not be recommended for those with documented yeast allergies or a history of an adverse reaction to the vaccine.

This is very worrying because if these vaccines are given to a baby on the day they are born, no one knows if:

- the baby has an allergy to yeast.

- the child has an allergy to any of the other vaccine ingredients."

"Families Pressured into Unnecessary Vaccines

U Thein Aung Zaw told reporters:

'We had no money for the vaccine, but the nurse urged me to protect my child, so I borrowed money for it. After my son was born, the doctor told me he was healthy and fine. By 8:30 pm they told me my son had died. They asked me if I wanted him buried in the hospital or if I wanted to take him back to my village. I couldn't afford what they were charging at the hospital, so I took my son's body to the village.' [14]

[14] https://healthimpactnews.com/2016/is-the-deadly-hepatitis-b-vaccine-more-dangerous-than-the-disease/ accessed Jan 2nd, 2019 @ 07:08

Aluminium Toxicity

This vaccine also contains aluminium, another ingredient that is causing concern. In 2012, a paper written by Stephanie Seneff, Robert M. Davidson and Jingjing Liu, titled _Empirical Data Confirm Autism Symptoms Related to Aluminium and Acetaminophen Exposure_, confirmed that exposure to a large number of vaccinations containing the adjuvant aluminium at a young age was the most likely cause for the increase in autism and other adverse reactions to vaccines. They wrote:

'In this paper, we have presented some analyses of the VAERS database which strongly suggest that the aluminium in vaccines is toxic to vulnerable children. While we have not shown that aluminum is directly causative in autism, the compelling evidence available from the literature on the toxicity of aluminium, combined with the evidence we present for severe adverse reactions occurring much more frequently following administration of aluminium-containing vaccines as compared to non-aluminium containing vaccines, suggests that neuronal damage due to aluminium penetration into the nervous system may be a significant factor in autism. The fact that mentions of autism rose steadily concomitant with significant increases in the aluminium burden in vaccines, is highly suggestive.'

This is particularly bad news to any parent considering having their children vaccinated, as a growing number of the childhood vaccinations now contain the adjuvant aluminium as an ingredient.

This was explained in depth by paediatrician Robert Sears, in his excellent article published in the magazine Mothering in 2008.

Dr. Sears is another professional exceptionally worried about the effects of aluminium on children's health. In an article warning mothers about the dangers of vaccinations containing the adjuvant, titled '*Is Aluminium The New Thimerosal?*' Dr. Sears explained that aluminium is added to vaccinations to help them work more efficiently.

He stated that although this would not normally be a problem because aluminium is a naturally occurring element found everywhere in our environment, including our food, water, air and soil, he had become worried about the effects that aluminium was having on children's health. He began to wonder if anyone had ever actually tested the safe level of injected aluminium.

During his research, he came across a number of extremely worrying documents. However, few were as worrying as the one written by the American Society for Parenteral and Enteral Nutrition (ASPEN). Describing the document in depth, Sears wrote:

'The source of the daily limit of 4 to 5mcg of aluminium per kilogram of body weight quoted by the ASPEN statement seems to be a study that compared the neurologic development of about 100 premature babies who were fed a standard IV solution that contained aluminium, with the development of 100 premature babies who were fed the same solution with almost all aluminium filtered out. The study was prompted by a number of established facts: that injected aluminium can build up to toxic levels in the bloodstream, bones, and brain; that preemies have decreased kidney function and thus a higher risk of toxicity; that an autopsy performed on one preemie whose sudden death was otherwise unexplained revealed high aluminium concentrations in the brain; and that aluminium toxicity can cause progressive dementia.'

He continued by giving some extremely alarming facts, of which few parents are aware:

'However, none of these documents or studies mentions vaccines; they look only at IV solutions and injectable medications. Nor does the FDA require labels on vaccines warning the public about the dangers of aluminium toxicity, although such labels are required for all other injectable medications. All of these studies and label warnings seem to apply mainly to premature babies and kidney patients. What about larger, full-term babies with healthy kidneys?'

He explained:

'These documents do not tell us what the maximum safe dose would be for a healthy baby or child, and I cannot find such information anywhere. This is probably why the ASPEN group suggests, and the FDA requires, that all injectable solutions be limited to 25mcg as we at least know that that level is safe.'

If this is so, then why do the recommended childhood vaccinations include far above the recommended amounts of aluminium? According to Dr. Sears, the levels of aluminium included in childhood vaccinations are as follows:

DTaP (diphtheria, tetanus, and pertussis): **170– 625mcg**, depending on manufacturer

hepatitis A: **250mcg**

hepatitis B: **250mcg**

Hib (for meningitis; PedVaxHib brand only): **225mcg**

HPV: 225mcg

Pediarix (DTaP–hepatitis B–polio combination): **850mcg**

Pentacel (DTaP–Hib–polio combination): **330mcg**

Pneumococcus: **125mcg** (emphasis added)

You do not have to be medically qualified to understand that these levels far exceed the safe levels recommended by ASPEN, especially when you consider that a newborn baby is vaccinated with the hepatitis B vaccine, containing 250mcg of aluminium, at birth!

In fact, according to Dr. Sears, the FDA stated that:

'Although aluminium toxicity is not commonly detected clinically, it can be serious in selected patient populations, such as **neonates (newborns)**, and may be more common than is recognised.'

If this is true, then why are all newborn babies, including those born prematurely, vaccinated at birth against hepatitis B, with a vaccine loaded with more than the recommended safe levels of aluminium?

For more information on Doctors Worldwide Express Concern about the Hepatitis B Vaccine

One doctor, who was pro-vaccine, the late _Dr. Bernadine Healy_, expressed her concern about infants receiving the hepatitis B vaccine. She, alongside other medical experts, was concerned about exposing infants to the vaccines' potential side effects at such an early age, unless the infant is at risk of contracting the disease.

Speaking to CBS News, Dr. Healy and her colleagues reasoned whether or not infants should be vaccinated at such an early age.

She stated:

'It's unnecessary to expose infants to this vaccine and its potential side effects at such an early age, unless they are at special risk for contracting the disease; most infants have no direct contact with body fluids of someone infected with hepatitis B, so what's the rush in exposing them to the series of vaccinations?'

Speaking to _VRAN_ (Vaccination Risk Awareness Network), Dr. Girard suggested that even in high-endemic countries, the risk/benefit ratio of what he described as 'this unusually toxic vaccine' must be carefully reassessed.

VRAN stated:

Dr. Girard recently disclosed evidence demonstrating that this specific vaccine is remarkable by the unusual frequency, severity and variety of its adverse events. He also reported that studies performed by the French Health Authorities that revealed clear auto-immune risks have remained unpublished.

Another organisation that is concerned that the hepatitis B vaccine is being given to all infants in the U.S. regardless as to whether or not they are at risk from the virus is the Children's Medical Safety Research Institute (_CMSRI_).

Claire Dwoskin, the founder of the organisation, wrote:

'So, what about the overwhelming majority of infants who won't engage in any of the activities that put individuals at risk for catching hepatitis B, or whose mothers have not tested positive for the disease? Does it still make sense to administer a hepatitis B vaccine in infancy?'

Additionally, the hepatitis B vaccine currently administered to infants was previously only recommended to adults who were at high risk for contracting the disease. However, because a large percentage of these high-risk individuals elected not to receive the vaccine, the government adopted an alternative approach to managing hepatitis B: universal administration. Thanks to the choices of a minority of high-risk individuals, now all children born in the U.S. must receive a vaccine at a time in which their immune systems are still fragile.

Conclusion

Clearly, there is much controversy surrounding the safety of the hepatitis B vaccination. Whether or not it was the vaccine itself that caused the outbreak of blood poisoning in Burma or unsanitary hospital conditions has not been officially determined. However, all vaccinations should be rigorously tested and proven to be safe and effective prior to recommendation. The vaccines must also be appropriately handled and administered by knowledgeable and competent medical professionals and when adverse reactions do occur, the staff must be trained to recognise the potential for vaccines to be the cause and be able to provide the necessary care to protect each valuable life.

Comment on this article at VaccineImpact.com" [15]

Let us hear what Dr. Andrew Moulden has to say.

"Dr. Andrew Moulden: Every Vaccine Produces Harm

Canadian physician Dr. Andrew Moulden provided clear scientific evidence to prove that every dose of vaccine given to a child or an adult produces harm. The truth that he uncovered was rejected by the conventional medical system and the pharmaceutical industry. Nevertheless, his warning and his message to America remain as a solid legacy of the man who stood up against big pharma and their program to vaccinate every person on the Earth.

---

[15] https://healthimpactnews.com/2016/is-the-deadly-hepatitis-b-vaccine-more-dangerous-than-the-disease/ accessed Jan 2nd, 2019 @ 07:33

Dr. Moulden died unexpectedly in November 2013 at age 49.

Because of the strong opposition from big pharma concerning Dr. Moulden's research, we became concerned that the name of this brilliant researcher and his life's work had nearly been deleted from the internet. His reputation was being disparaged, and his message of warning and hope was being distorted and buried without a tombstone. This book summarizes his teaching and is a must-read for everyone who wants to learn the 'other side' of the vaccine debate that the mainstream media routinely censors.

Read Dr. Andrew Moulden: Every Vaccine Produces Harm on your mobile device or computer, by ordering the eBook!" [16]

I don't know what to think of all of this. Do you?

I do not feel that I am a critic. I do not feel that I am scaremongering either, but everywhere I look, I see these reports and facts of the dangers of vaccines and immunizations. How are the vaccines getting

---

[16] https://eclinik.net/every-vaccine-produces-harm-dr-andrew-moulden/ accessed Jan 2nd, 2019 @ 07:35

FDA approval? Or are all these stories and expert analyses incorrect?

I know there is a lot of money in both the wellness and pharmaceutical industries and the money seems to be in the **PREVENTION** and not the **CURE** of illnesses, which does not sit right with me.

I DON'T LIKE THIS.

IT IS OUR CHILDREN'S LIVES, SOULS AND BODIES WHICH ARE ON THE LINE!

I am no expert in these fields.

And I am not saying that vaccinations are bad for us. There are many advocates.

All I can say is that no one has died from smoking **MARIJUANA,** and it is deemed to be very bad, despite its known health benefits. I wish I could say the same about vaccinations.

I just wanted to share my mind with you on this as I have seen, heard and experienced issues with vaccinations and have even had a few **MAJOR** incidences within the family, despite all the good things that people have been saying.

CHAPTER 5:

THINGS

I n past times, the prerequisite was affording basic needs, such as food, shelter, and **LOVE**. We didn't care if we had the new Xbox or PlayStation or the new Nike Air Jordan's or that new shiny fast car or new sofa. If we had these things, it was very much appreciated, but if we didn't, then we appreciated the little we had. We **ALWAYS** made things work, without excuses, without blaming it on a lack of this or a lack of that.

Often people blame lack of material possessions for stopping them from achieving their goals or arriving at their destinations. This appears to be the trend these days. What do you think?

Many people today are still suffering. Or so it would seem?

People of today still appear to be suffering, even though affording basic needs is no longer a problem.

However, if we really analyze the **ROOT CAUSE** of this suffering we speak of, we would find that it has been **SELF-CREATED**.

THINK about it, please?

If it is not a necessity, then **WE** do not really **NEED** it. **WE** may **LIKE**, **WANT** or **DESIRE** it, but if it is something other than the fulfillment of a **BASIC NEED**, **WE** do not **NEED** it. **WE** should instill this concept into our **CHILDREN**.

This is just my humble point of view.

What are your thoughts?

You see, **WE** seem to suffer because we want things that do not add value to our lives. We have a roof over our heads, and in most cases, at least enough money for us to work on our passion(s). But surprisingly, we are sad because we do not have luxurious gadgets to keep us up to date with others around us.

Please check out the following article:

"Reasons Why We Suffer

1. We want more than enough

Most of us suffer because we want things that do not add value to our lives. We have a roof over our heads and enough money for us to work on our passion, but surprisingly, we are sad, because we do not have some luxurious gadgets that never add value to our lives.

The media, through movies, music, and advertise-ments have lied to us that our happiness depends on the number of things we own.

This lie has made people, who have enough money to be richer than half of the world's population, to believe that they are inadequate, just because they do not own the luxuries that the rich and famous possess.

This feeling of inadequacy has led to mental illnesses such as depression and _anxiety_, hence resulting in suffering.

In addition, we fail to understand that we don't have to worry about possessing luxurious products because the only thing we have to do is work hard, and these things shall follow.

2. Attachment to the ungraspable

Another factor that results in our suffering is attaching ourselves to temporary things such as our material possessions.

Most of us attach ourselves deeply to our material possessions because we love them so much. We fail to realize the fact that these things are temporary. For instance, they are vulnerable to theft or destruction, and so we can lose them anytime.

We are not conscious of the fact that identifying ourselves with these possessions ensures that we suffer. For example, you fail to realize that the frustration that arises after losing your phone occurs because you have identified yourself with the gadget. Therefore, to avoid suffering we must release our attachments to temporary things and only identify ourselves with divine intelligence, which is a permanent source of wealth and happiness.

3. Not Realising that the source of creation dwells in us

Most of us believe that we are physical beings without any value on this earth. We fail to realize that we are spiritual beings living in human bodies and that we are Gods because the divine intelligence exists in us.

We do not realize that the divine intelligence in us is what takes part in enabling our bodies to perform bodily functions such as digestion, breathing, or blood circulation.

If we reflect on the fact that the divine intelligence exists in us, we will never suffer our hardships because we will realize that we have the power to overcome all the challenges that life throws at us. This knowledge also ensures that we are free from suffering because it makes us realize that we have enough wisdom in life to deal with our circumstances.

Therefore, we have to realize that we are Gods and that the problems we face only appear as problems because we ignore the fact that the Creator's spirit exists in us. Thus, what appears as a problem must not make you suffer because it is nothing compared to who we are.

4. Comparing ourselves to others

Today, most of us love comparing ourselves with others, hence bringing stress in our lives because there are some people who will always be better than us.

For instance, no matter how much money you earn, there will always be some friends who will be making a higher amount than you. Also, no matter how good looking you are, there will always be people who are better looking than you.

Comparing ourselves to others leads to suffering because it makes us care so much about people's opinions about us. Therefore, to avoid suffering, we must avoid comparing ourselves with others, and we must only concentrate on checking our progress by assessing where we are today and comparing our current situation with who we were yesterday." [17]

This is an excellent article by Isaac, a Kenyan entrepreneur, professional research writer, and founder of *www.unboundedwisdom.com*. He loves

[17] https://www.successconsciousness.com/blog/letting-go/reasons-why-we-suffer/ accessed Jan 3rd, 2019 @ 06:03

sharing ideas related to success and spirituality, and he likes enlightening people on the factors that could help them live a happy and successful life. He pretty much sums up everything that I wanted to say on this matter.

The only point that I feel like re-emphasizing is his 3rd point, and I STRONGLY ADVISE that we INSTIL this fact, INGRAIN this fact into THE MIND of OUR CHILDREN.

The FACT that THEY are CREATORS!

THEY are THE CREATORS of the NEW WORLD.

They are OUR future GODS AND GODDESSES.

They should know this. If we get this part right, it will most definitely make the world a better place.

Before you say the world is a bad place and things are out of **YOUR CONTROL** or **OUR CONTROL,** please **THINK** about it. The next time you say **WHAT CAN WE DO?** please **THINK** about it. Next time we are feeling that **WE CANNOT DO NOTHING, WE SHOULD DO SOMETHING.**

REMEMBER THE WORLD IS OURS, AND OUR CHILDREN HOLD THE KEYS TO THE FUTURE!

LET US MAKE A NICE FUTURE FOR OUR GOLDEN ONES. LET US GIVE THEM THE RIGHT KNOWLEDGE, RIGHT WISDOM AND RIGHT OVERSTANDING!

CHAPTER 6:

PERSONAS

The world is constantly evolving. Life is progressively evolving. Changes are occurring.

Social media is strong and plenty. Computers are everywhere.

We have super fast **Wi-Fi** (wireless internet), and we can video call anywhere.

Life is such a dream. But is it?

I love all this technology, but I love nature too. If we have a good balance in our lives and a good sense of maturity, then we stand a good chance of not being violated, manipulated or abused. You can never get too much nature, but too much technology can always be a problem — especially if not handled in the appropriate manner.

Now the online world is a crazy place and **WE ALL** need to be aware and careful.

We need to realize that when we are using the internet (especially social media):

• All of our browsing histories can be unearthed and traced back to us — anything from a drunken, half-naked photo to an angry rant on a political website. Keywords are powerful things, and most people have no idea how to cover their online tracks. We should always be vigilant. So should our children. There are no **SECRETS** online, so we need to be careful about what **WE PUBLISH**. Once things go **PUBLIC,** they go **PUBLIC,** and **WHEN** things go **LIVE,** they go **LIVE!**

- Online bullying is rife, especially amongst "**schoolies.**" We **need** to **take responsibility** for the online activity of **OUR CHILDREN** in order to **GUIDE, NURTURE** and **PROTECT** them. We will probably learn a lot too.

- We need not forget about personalized advertising, which seems to be based on our online activity, suggestively coercing us to spend money on the things that we like. **THEY GET TO KNOW US?**

- Who are our online friends?

- Who are friends with **OUR CHILDREN** online, and what is their **RELATIONSHIP?**

- We all have the issue of our **online persona** (identity) **vs** our **real persona** to consider and deal with.

What is an online persona?

Please see below:

"**Internet Identity (IID),** also **online identity** or **internet persona**, is a *social identity* that an Internet user establishes in online communities and websites. It can also be considered as an actively constructed presentation of oneself. Although some people choose to use their real names online, some Internet users prefer to be anonymous, identifying themselves by means of pseudonyms, which reveal varying amounts of *personally identifiable information*. An online identity may even be determined by a user's relationship to a certain social group they are a part of online. Some can even be deceptive about their identity.

In some online contexts, including Internet forums, online chats, and *massively multiplayer online role-playing games* (MMORPGs), users can represent themselves visually by choosing an avatar, an icon-sized graphic image. Avatars are one-way users express their online identity. Through interaction with other users, an established online identity acquires a *reputation*, which enables other users to decide whether the identity is worthy of *trust*. Online identities are associated with users through *authentication*, which typically requires *registration* and *logging in*. Some websites also use the user's *IP address* or *tracking cookies* to identify users.

The concept of the self, and how this is influenced by emerging technologies, are a subject of research in fields such as education, psychology and sociology.

The *online disinhibition effect* is a notable example, referring to a concept of unwise and uninhibited behavior on the Internet, arising as a result of anonymity and audience gratification.

Online Social Identity

Identity Expression and Identity Exposure

See also: Online Identity Management and Impression Management

The social web, termed as the usage of the web to support the social process, represents a space in which people have the possibility to *express* and expose their identity in a social context. For example, people define their identity explicitly by creating *user profiles* in *social network services* such as *Facebook* or *LinkedIn* and *online dating services*. By expressing opinions on *blogs* and other social media, they define more tacit *identities*.

The disclosure of a person's identity may present certain issues related to *privacy*. Many people adopt strategies that help them control the disclosure of their personal information online. Some strategies require users to invest considerable effort.

The emergence of the concept of online identity has raised many questions among academics. *Social networking services* and online *avatars* have complicated the concept of identity. Academia has responded to these emerging trends by establishing domains of scholarly research such as self-studies, which focuses on all aspects of human identity in technological societies.

Online activities may affect our offline personal identity, as well." [18]

With all this in mind, it is vital that we are **FULLY AWARE** and **MONITOR** what image we are portraying online and for what reason and what the impact will be. **IS IT THE REAL ME?** How different is my online persona to the real me? **WHAT IMAGE IS MY CHILD PORTRAYING ONLINE? WHAT SECURITY MEASURES HAVE I PUT IN PLACE FOR MY CHILD'S ONLINE ACTIVITY?**

Children have been known to flaunt themselves on the likes of Facebook, Instagram, Snapchat, etc. They all

[18] Unknown

would like to be stars and out-there on their own platforms, wallowing in self-glorification. But are they **LIKE THIS** in **REAL LIFE?** Most are not.

Maybe this was the **PLAN** all along, who knows?

What we need to realize is that there are many complexities to this life that we are living. **Do OUR CHILDREN know who they really are?**

Do WE know who we really are? I guess that would be a good place to start.

You are probably reading this thinking: **"BAA** humbug." I am sorry if you feel that way. I just felt that these words needed to be **DELIVERED**.

It is what it is.

CHAPTER 7:

THE MATRIX

N o, this is not a movie. It is real. What is real? Are we not all living in our own realities? This is confusing to me.

They say that we are living in a matrix. I feel so. What about you?

What is this matrix that we speak?

Is it the complex social condition, environment and structure in which we the people live our lives, with the wires all crossing each other?

Is it a spell, sickness or incarceration which keeps us locked into a **3D** perspective of person, places and things, with no knowledge of self?

Who knows? Do You?

Let us see or hear what a few of the experts are saying:

"Elon Musk, the billionaire entrepreneur and founder of Space X, Tesla and PayPal, has told The Telegraph, ['There is only a one in billions chance that we're not living in a computer simulation.']" [19]

---

[19] https://www.telegraph.co.uk/technology/2016/06/03/we-are-almost-definitely-living-in-a-matrix-style-simulation-cla/ accessed Dec 30th, 2019 @ 09:13

"Very low-frequency version: Rape and abuse. High frequency: I surrender. The mind and heart are absent in the **Matrix** version and that is why porn sells, and that is one of the reasons they don't give you a working road map. On a higher note, the statement represents all that the sacred feminine spirit is all about: 'Surrendering and nurturing.'

Sexuality is a feeling, not a thought process, and since sexuality has been very much intellectualised by the Matrix, that should be one good reason to climb out of that bed. In a way, the caveman attitude towards sex is more honest than today's mainstream sexuality, since it came without agendas or power play." [20]

"In his paper, Dr. Bostrom suggested a race of far-evolved descendants could be behind our digital imprisonment.

'The futuristic beings – human or otherwise – could be using virtual reality to simulate a time in the past or recreate how their remote ancestors lived.'

---

[20] https://www.davidicke.com/article/499225/sexuality-missing-coordinates accessed Dec 30th, 2019 @ 09:13 @ 09:18

Sound crazy? Well, it turns out NASA thinks Dr. Bostrom might be right." [21]

"Some of the world's richest and most powerful people are convinced that we are living in a computer simulation. And now they're trying to do something about it.

At least two of Silicon Valley's tech billionaires are pouring money into efforts to break humans out of the simulation that they believe that they are living in, according to a new report.

Philosophers have long been concerned about how we can know that our world isn't just a very believable simulation of a real one. But concern about that has become ever more active in recent years, as computers and artificial intelligence have advanced." [22]

I am not an expert, but it is obvious that there is something going on, and I feel that if we are to escape this **MATRIX** or whatever you would like to call all this

[21] http://www.theeventchronicle.com/galactic/nasa-scientist-says-we-may-be-living-in-a-matrix-like-digital-imprisonment-designed-by-aliens/ accessed Dec 30th, 2018 @ 09:36

[22] https://www.independent.co.uk/life-style/gadgets-and-tech/news/computer-simulation-world-matrix-scientists-elon-musk-artificial-intelligence-ai-a7347526.html accessed Dec 30th, 2018 @ 09:44

stuff (which no one seems to acknowledge?), it would help if we looked into the following, especially for the sake of **OUR CHILDREN**.

This is just my humble opinion. Please do not be offended.

TIME, I feel, is the main element of the matrix; most people are *imprisoned* by time, *chasing* time, *losing* time, *worrying* about time.

We should realize that **TIME** is just an **ILLUSION**. Back in the day, there was no time, and everything was sweet: things worked, people still worked things out. I think it's best that we teach this lesson to our children as **TIME** is nothing but a tool to keep us locked into this **3D** reality in which we are currently living our **LIVES**.

"We **LIVED** by **TIME** like a **DEVIL** in **HELL**." – Dr Kwadw(o) Naya: Baa Ankh Em Ra A'lyun Eil

Whoever created this time malarkey has done an excellent job of mentally enslaving the planet. What do you think?

MONEY is not **THE WORLD**, and that is what **OUR CHILDREN** need to know. I see so many **innocent souls** *taken* for their **LOVE** of **MONEY**. It is not very nice. This point should be firmly instilled into the very being of our **GOLDEN ONES.**

"Money is the oil that greases life, but it is not life; therefore, we should never exchange or sell our soul for it." – Dr Kwadw(o) Naya: Baa Ankh Em Ra A'lyun Eil

Sadly, it is commonplace these days. We all need to realize that money is just a financial tool which is used as a medium of exchange. How many people have you seen manipulated into doing things which are against their better nature for **MONEY**?

LOVE IS THE HIGHEST FORM OF BEING. In this 3D physical world or realm that most of us are mentally trapped, we live between two polarities. **LOVE** and **HATE**. At present, it looks like the world is being run by hate. How many times do we turn our televisions on to see some hate going on somewhere in the world? How many times do we see **LOVE**?

SERVICE & SERVITUDE are the keys to humanity. We should all know that, and we should bring our children up with these very same ideals. We should all live for ourselves, but we should also live for one another. Wouldn't this make the world a better place?

Instead of hating on people who do well, would it not be better to support these people? You never know... when they make it, they may serve us back.

If people are trying to bust out of the matrix, wouldn't it be a better idea to help them rather than hold them back or call them mad or crazy?

KNOWLEDGE gives us power. With the right knowledge, we have the power to provide and do the right thing for ourselves and our families.

POWER is very important to **US;** each man and woman is gifted with their own unique powers and strengths. **WE** the **PEOPLE** should never give our powers away without consent, and we should be very very careful before doing so if we do choose to do so. Try to be more aware so as to not be manipulated or tricked. It is a funny world out there, and there are many snakes. If we are going to break free from this *MIND PRISON* or **THIS WORLD OF ILLUSION,** we are going to need our power.

UNITY is most important. Collective powers are obviously greater than individual powers. As you can **IMAGINE**, together, we can achieve a lot. Can we be played, manipulated or deceived if we join together in **COMMON-UNITY,** like the **COMMUNITIES** of old times?

CHAPTER 8:

FEEDING THE HUNGER

We need to feed our children correctly. At the moment, they are being *overfed*, *underfed*, *diseased*, *malnourished* and sometimes even given *fake* or *bad food*.

We **LOVE** our **CHILDREN,** don't **WE**?

When I refer to **FOOD** in this instance, I am referring to what we **FEED** our children.

Nowadays, our children are **FED** with *lies*, *fairy tales* and often *spookism*, but **WHY**?

This is not right, surely?

Our children are **STARVING** here!

Or MALNOURISHED!

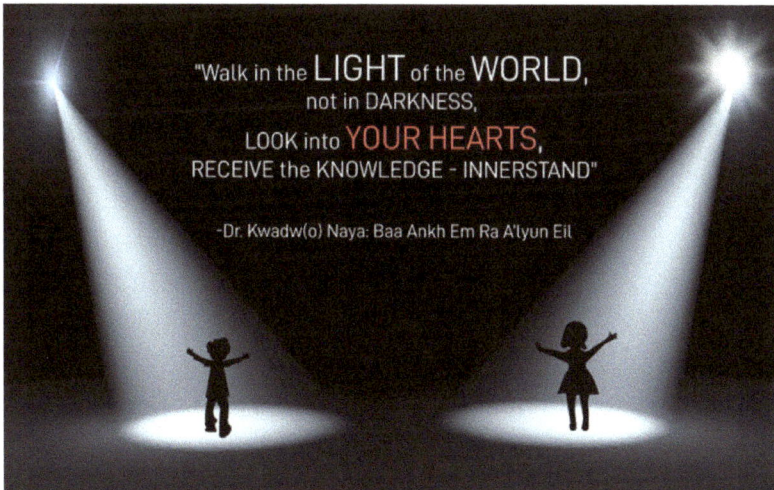

"Walk in the LIGHT of the WORLD, not in DARKNESS, LOOK into YOUR HEARTS, RECEIVE the KNOWLEDGE - INNERSTAND"

-Dr. Kwadw(o) Naya: Baa Ankh Em Ra A'lyun Eil

They're so busy being fed **FAKE** things that many children have no time for nature. They tend to lean more towards transhumanism. You never know, the next set of children may be able to **MORPH** into their Xbox or PlayStation. Who knows? I would opt for **spiritual transformation** any day of the week.

WHICH WOULD YOU CHOOSE?

WE Humans? Programs? Machines? Earthians? Animals? I don't really know what to call **US, DO YOU?**

We need to **FEED** the **MIND, BODIES** and **SOULS** of **OUR CHILDREN** with the correct **FUEL** so that they can achieve the **OPTIMUM** that this **LIFE** can give them.

WE ALL KNOW WHAT TO DO, DON'T WE?

I know that there is no **right** or *wrong* as it is down to perception, but many people do not do the right thing at all. They might do the right thing for them, but not the **RIGHT** thing. This life is full of contradictions.

But please do not be a *DEVIL*. We may have **LIVED** as a *DEVIL,* but it doesn't mean we need to raise our kids the same. To **LIVE** can be *EVIL* if done the **WRONG way**. Can you imagine a world full of *devils*? A group of girls all gyrating, leading the men astray saying "girls, girls, we run the world" or the boys running around saying "any holes a goal." Is this the future that we would like to push?

GODLINESS IS NEXT TO CLEANLINESS!

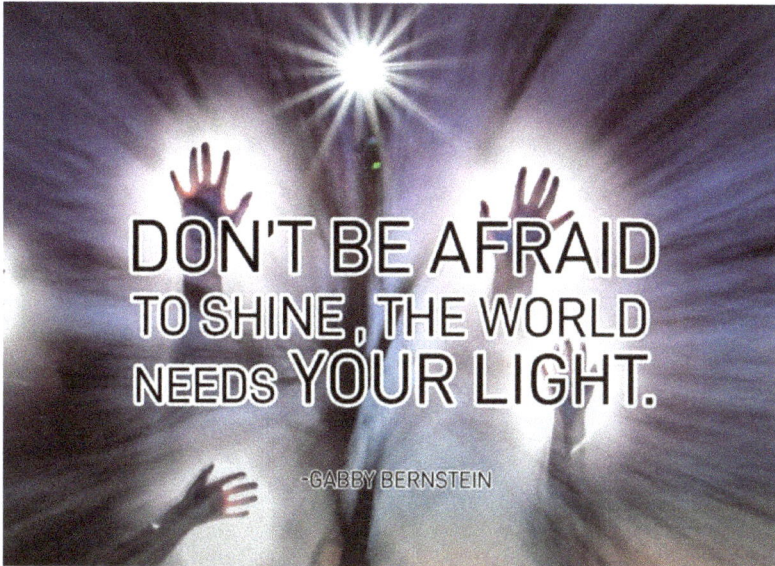

Why can we not raise our children to be Gods and Goddesses, likened after PURENESS AND CLEANLINESS?

CHAPTER 9:

THE HOLY TRINITY

W hen I was young, my sister and I **HAD** to attend church.

Northgate United Reformed Church in Darlington (U.K.) was the one.

The pastors were very nice, and **MOST** of the people were really nice. However, the information that I received didn't resonate with my being, I am sorry to say.

My father is a Bishop. So, maybe I shouldn't be speaking like this, but this is how I feel.

I am not religious or anti-religious. I just **AM.**

So many times, I have been taught that the holy trinity relates to Father, Son and the Holy Ghost, but this has never really made much sense to me. How is that the Holy Trinity? Can someone explain it to me, please?

It seems to equate to a male-dominated world. What is this? Father, Son and Holy Ghost: Holy Trinity or Holy Smoke?

I still don't get it. I don't get church, really: nice people singing the same old songs every week but going out and doing bad stuff over the weekend and praying and repenting on Sundays. This never made any sense to me. Why are we singing these boring songs every week and saying these boring prayers? Is it to put us to sleep? Do not get me wrong... there were some great people, who had great intentions and heart, but it was not for me. I felt that I needed more.

I was very happy when I saw the real Holy Trinity, courtesy of Dr. Malachi Z York. He really did show me the way.

Holy Trinity Crucifix
... powerful visual of the mystery of the Holy Trinity, this crucifix depicts God the Father, God the Son, and God the Holy Spirit, all supporting one another. A beautiful crucifix to display as a reminder of this central profession of Christian faith. Blessed Trinity wall crucifix A special piece...

23

I saw this today, and it brought back a few memories.

We were always taught about the cross at school and how it relates to the Holy Trinity. They say that the **Holy Spirit** is the love **between** the Father and the Son and that the Father loved the Son so much that he let him die on a cross to save all of our sins.

We were taught that **Jesus** died to take on himself the penalty for our **sins**. God's son, the second person of the **Holy Trinity**, paid for all our sins by taking our place. On the **cross**, **Jesus** took our **sins,** so God could give Christ consciousness to those who believe in him.

_____

[23] https://search.catholiccompany.com/catholic/Holy-trinity-cross accessed Dec 28th, 2018 @ 12:30

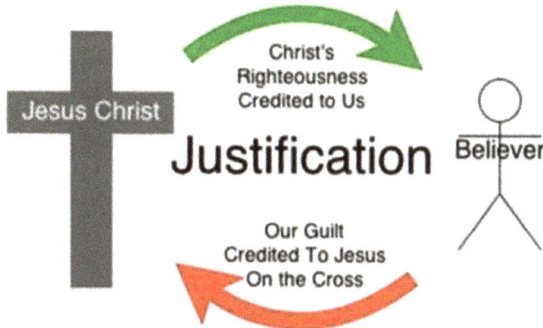

Source: [24]

What is this Holy Trinity?

"The Holy Trinity is part of many sects of Christian doctrine. The belief is that God is of three parts: God the Father; God the Son, as represented by Christ; and God the Holy Spirit. The key element of this belief is that God is at once a single God, but also that each aspect of him is individual.

For some, the Holy Trinity represents polytheism and is therefore not in keeping with the concept of one God. Those who believe in the Trinity insist this is not a polytheistic view, but it is part of God's mystery that he presents as three discrete persons in one joined God.

[24] http://3.bp.blogspot.com/k6PVo3inEiw/VhVOgqrrNRI/AAAAAAASVY/GSRBvnqRABc/s1600/double%2Bimputation.jpg accessed Dec 28th, 2018 @ 14:00

Each part has its own will and personality, but each is also a part of the other. It is a rather difficult concept to understand for those unfamiliar with Christian doctrine. It is thought of by most as part of the mystery of God.

The teaching of the Holy Trinity is often a dynamic process, and views on the Trinity tend to change. Women who wish for greater roles in the church often describe the Holy Spirit as feminine in nature, though there is not much scriptural basis for doing so. There is still a huge theological debate on how to perceive the Trinity, or whether to discard the traditional understanding of it.

In Eastern Orthodox Churches, the debate about the Holy Trinity is ongoing, with some questioning whether the idea was taken from pantheistic religions in order to make Christianity more palatable, or whether it is the most accurate depiction of God. The resolution of this discussion might result in the unification of the churches most similar to Roman Catholic Churches, but with several hundred years of discussion on this topic, this is yet to occur." [25]

It all sounds **"hairy fairy"** to me. Does anyone know what is going on?

---

[25] https://www.wisegeek.com/what-is-the-holy-trinity.htm accessed Dec 28th, 2018 @ 12:51

I do not intend to insult or provoke anyone. This is just my humble view.

Now let us have a look at the cross.

The symbol of the cross became immensely popular in Christian art and funerary monuments from around century 350. Christian devotion to the **cross** centered on the victory of Christ over the powers of evil and death.

The cross today is often seen as a representation of the instrument of the crucifixion of Jesus and is the best-known symbol used and wore, not just by Christians. But the realistic portrayal of his suffering is not often considered?

THIS IS WHAT I THINK OF THE HOLY TRINITY IN WHICH I WAS BROUGHT UP WITH (NO OFFENCE):

I don't know if it is good thinking or bad. I will leave you to be the judge.

I just read an interesting post by Mischelle Milton on her Facebook, which funnily enough coincides with what we have just been discussing:

Mischelle Milton

"The cross is a promotion for paedophilia and death.

The Ankh cross represents the feminine and the masculine rebirth, eternal life and the union of male and female. You cannot destroy energy... only the physical form. Energy can only transform. It never dies. It's infinity!

That cross you so proudly wear, and praise represents death. Why do you think there is an image of your dead Jesus on it? It has nothing to do with life or eternity."

#Facts [26]

---

[26] Accessed Dec 28th, 2018 @ 12:53

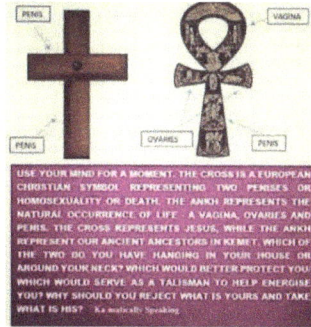

Source: [27] (Remember King James was an open homosexual)

I have heard many people speak of such things like this, and it does kind of make sense. Many people say that the Ankh is the **real** cross which represents the **real** Holy Trinity, but who am I to say?

They say that the Ankh is an ancient symbol of fertility which represents the man and woman coming together to create a child. They also refer to the Ankh as the key to life. I must admit this concept does make a little bit more sense than the God, Son and Holy Spirit ideology. At least women do come into play in this line of thinking.

[27] https://www.facebook.com/search/str/the+cross+and+the+ankh/keywords_search?epa=SEARCH_BOX accessed Dec 28th, 2018 @ 14:35

ANKH - Sign of Life

"The 'Sign of Life was regarded as a powerful symbol during the times of the Pharaohs, rulers of Ancient Egyptian dynasty.

I discreetly took this picture during a visit to the Mummy Exhibition. I found it rather intriguing and ironic, considering that death is the main subject with Mummy!

Faience amulet in the shape of *Ankh,* said to be from Gebel Barkal, Egypt, 25th Dynasty to Late Period, about 700-500 BC. This amulet was acquired by Lord Kitchener in Sudan. It probably originated in a temple, since amulets found in burials are usually smaller." – Amy Lam [28]

Please let me know your thoughts.

---

[28] https://amylamsg.com/2013/05/10/ankh/ accessed Dec 28th, 2018 @ 15:11

ANKH
The Kemetic Womb of Mankind and Eternal Life

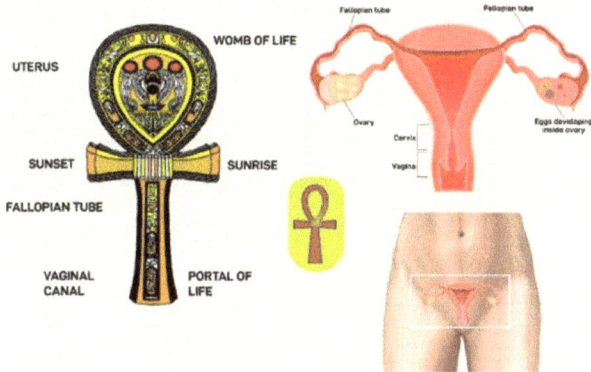

THE TRUE MYSTERY OF THE ANKH REVEALED
THE MALE AND FEMALE REPRODUCTIVE ORGANS COMBINED

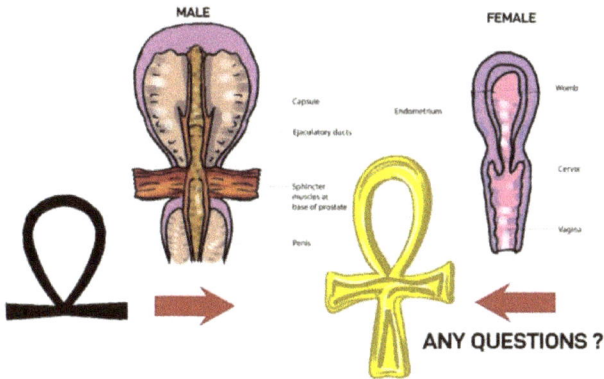

ANY QUESTIONS ?

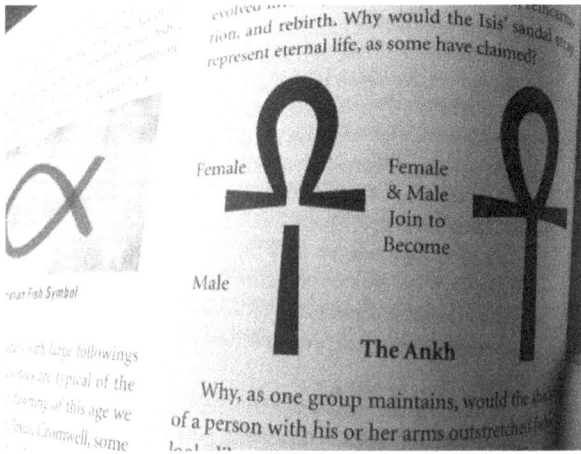

Source: [29]

I am sure you get the gist, right?

The Ankh has been in existence for as long as I know. I did come across this image and it quite intrigued me so I thought that I would share it with you. I do not know much about it really, but it looks old. Maybe you can ENIGHTEN me?

[29] https://i.pinimg.com/originals/70/7e/7e/707e7e86dd c8fe4f56eb7acba3e237ef.jpg accessed Dec 28th, 2018 @ 14:58

Source: [30]

I suggest you check out Nuta Ankh's Blog when you get time. He has covered the Ankh in almost its entirety. It is a very interesting read:

https://nuta-ankh.blogspot.com/2014/04/ankh-kemetic-womb-of-mandkind-and.html

From a spiritual perspective, the Ankh really does seem to represent fertility, the key to life, and also the key to hidden knowledge.

Its loop symbolizes the eternal soul which has no beginning or end because it is energy and consciousness or

---

[30] https://www.facebook.com/photo.php?fbid=10698528 0371165&set=p.106985280371165&type=3&theater accessed Dec 28th, 2018 @ 21:01

unconsciousness or both. In any case, we all know that energy cannot be destroyed. Many people (myself, **now** included) feel that the Ankh is the key to unraveling the mysteries of life and death and thereafter.

The cross, on the other hand, appears to spiritually interpret and represent death, pain, betrayal and double-crossing. But for some reason, it is one of the most popular items used for jewelry and protection. I really don't understand it. I used to wear a cross. I had cross earrings and a cross necklace. I do not wear crosses anymore. As soon as I got the correct knowledge (correct in my eyes), I was done.

Dr.malachi z york

The Cross Can Be Found In Two Places, One On Top Of The Churchs, And The Other On Top Of The Grave, The One On To Of The Churchs Is Where The Mentalty Dead Are, And The One On Top Of The Grave Is, Where The Physical Dead Lav.

'LIFE)   (DEATH)

LIFEandDEATH
ANKHandCROSS

I cannot speak for you, so I am not sure what your take is on all of this, but if I was given a choice out of the Ankh and the Cross, I know which one I would choose.

Which one would you choose?

CONCLUSION

T alent is one of the best ways to change the world. With unique and outstanding talents, we can achieve greater heights in unimaginable ways. Everyone is attracted to talent because of its significance. In truth, every single child is gifted and talented in a specific area. We need to all realize that.

Our children need to be nurtured and trained in the right direction — one that will help them achieve whatever goal they set.

We are talking about our children here. It is important to note that education is of key relevance and a chief point of reference for managing children. Our sons and daughters need to be nurtured and guided; they also deserve a good start and a chance to become great in the future. It is all in our hands.

Nurturing a child is not easy. It requires a combination of effort, focus and good education.

Now the question is, "How do we help our children to be the best version of themselves that they can be?"

That's how we need to be thinking.

Our children are the future. If we have no children, we have no future, and if we raise bad children, then we are responsible for participating in the **CREATION** of a **BAD FUTURE! LET US MAKE THIS WORLD A BETTER PLACE!**

Why can't we help our children go on to achieve GREAT things and forget about **DISTRACTIONS** and **VICES**? Wouldn't it be better if WE ALL had a GREAT story to TELL?

Please look out for Choices 2

You can pre-order your own copy for only $1.30 here on Amazon (for a limited period only):

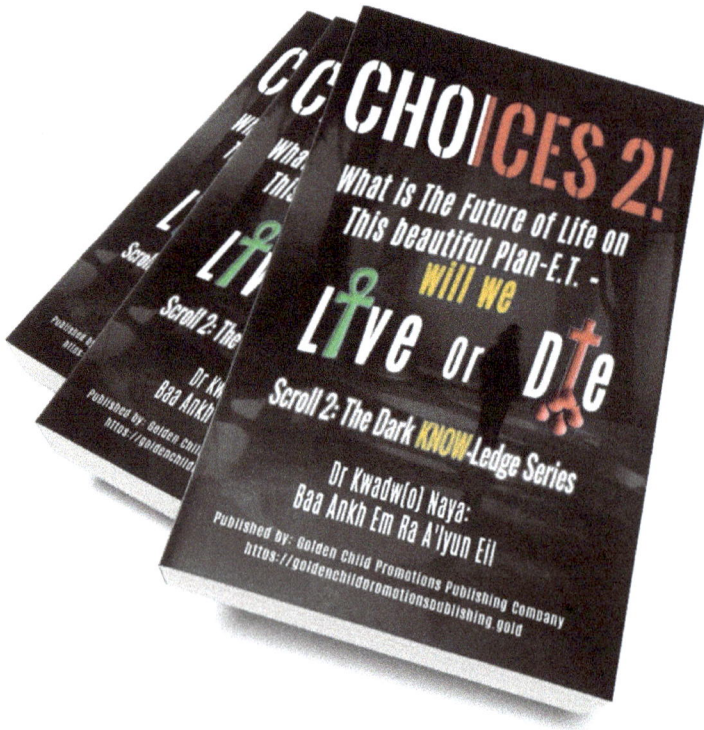

https://www.amazon.com/dp/B084611YYT?ref_=pe_3
052080_276849420

AFTERWARD

T his is my first attempt at writing a book. Thank you for being with me. It has been a pleasure.

I am 43 and have been on a journey, just like the rest of us. I remember all my childhood experiences, and that has made me who I am today. It has molded me, fashioned, shaped and formed me, and made me the very man that I am today.

I just wanted to take this opportunity to try and share my mind on some of the things that are happening today which have caused me concern, especially as I can truly relate to what we speak about today from personal experiences. Often, it has taken me a while to work things out. I didn't have great guidance. My parents taught me what was taught to them. Knowledge was scarce in those days. But it is all out there now — courtesy of the **NEW DIGITAL ERA**.

We have no excuses. If we really love our children, we would always do our best for them. We may not necessarily give them what they want or what is popular, but we will make the right choice, the best choice, and the true choice. When you look at things in this way, you will find that your options are very simple.

If anything is **detrimental to me,** then I would never wish it on my **CHILDREN.** I am sure you are all with me on this one.

Considering the fact that soul and spirit have no gender and also the fact that we are ALL made up of 102 minerals which come from the earth, a scientifically proven fact. WE come from the earth (NATURE) and WE return to the earth, (our physical body that is). What I am trying to say in a nutshell is that on the grand scheme of things we are all different but all equal, all different but all the same and WE ARE ALL ONE as we are ALL a PART of the ALL. THIS IS THE ONLY WAY I KNOW! NO ONE WILL SUCCEED INTER-GALACTICALLY or even on this PLAN-E.T. as an INDIVIDUAL as these traits and approaches to LIFE tend to support the EGO opposed to eradicating it. How can one be SAD when their CHILD or PARTNER DIES and not bat an eyelid when 400 women go missing in Nigeria, when thousand of people get blown up in Yemen or when all the good world leaders are been occultly eradicated (seemingly so), more often than not under suspicious circumstances which do not add up. PEACE, LOVE and HAPPINESS.....STAY SAFE and STAY HAPPY!

Thank you once again.

See you soon, ladies and gentlemen!

Hopefully I will catch you up in the next instalment:

Why I Know You Don't Love Your Children, scroll 2, which will be available very soon, please look out for it. If you would like to be one of the 1st to receive a free promotional copy, please email us @ *9x9x9@golden childpromotionspublishing.co.uk* with your name and contact details (specifying your request).

All the proceeds of this book will be donated to The Golden Child Promotions Charity, to fund youth development

https://goldenchildpromotions.co.uk

Thank You

Dr Kwadw(o) Naya: Baa Ankh Em Ra A'lyun Eil

ABOUT THE AUTHOR

Dr Kwadw(o) Naya: Baa Ankh Em Ra A'lyun Eil

Born: Catterick Garrison, UK

Nationality: British

Race: Negroid/Nubunin

Genre: Non-Fiction

Notable awards: PHD In Life and a master's in business as well as many other vocational qualifications.

Dr Kwadw(o) Naya: Baa Ankh Em Ra A'lyun Eil is an Author, Director, Mentor and Life Coach ('Transformational'), he is a new gentleman on the scene, one of the most promising newcomers for 2019.

He was born in a country where he has never been accepted, raised in a broken poverty-stricken home, which he was thrown out at the age of 15 never to return. Surprisingly he has had a very good career,

NOT GREAT, and is educated to master's level with 'degrees' in street knowledge. Despite his successes there has always been some unseen FORCES working against him, which he is only too happy to share.

Somehow, he has excelled with everything that he has touched and is not afraid of CHANGE, moving from running his own estate agency in the capital city of London (UK) to becoming a fully established author, mentor and life coach.

Dr Kwadw(o) Naya: Baa Ankh Em Ra A'lyun Eil is ready to share his KNOWLEDGE, WISDOM, and OVERSTANDING with YOU ALL.

He has written 20 books to date, please watch out for his works.

www.ingramcontent.com/pod-product-compliance
Lightning Source LLC
Chambersburg PA
CBHW041215030426
42336CB00023B/3356